THE NATIONAL
GEM COLLECTION

THE NATIONAL GEM COLLECTION

JEFFREY E. POST

WITH PHOTOGRAPHS BY CHIP CLARK

NATIONAL MUSEUM OF NATURAL HISTORY, SMITHSONIAN INSTITUTION

IN ASSOCIATION WITH

HARRY N. ABRAMS, INC., PUBLISHERS

Editor: Eric Himmel

Designer: Carol Robson

Front cover: The Gachala Emerald is a 858-carat uncut natural crystal from Gachala, Colombia. Resting on it is a 99.82-carat fluorite gem from South Africa. In front of it, from left to right: a 34.07 spinel from Mogok, Burma; a 52.26-carat calcite gem from Balmat, New York; and a 17.85-carat diamond crystal from Murfreesboro, Arkansas. Gifts of Harry Winston (emerald) and Kenji Kawaoka (fluorite)

Back cover: This 181.9-carat white opal was found in Coober Pedy, Australia

Photographs by Chip Clark © 1997 The National Museum of Natural History, Smithsonian Institution

Library of Congress Cataloging-in-Publication Data

National Museum of Natural History (U.S.)
    The national gem collection / Jeffrey E. Post; with photographs by Chip Clark.
        p.   cm.
    Includes index.
    ISBN 0–8109–3690–9 (clothbound) / 0–8109–2758–6 (paperback)
    1. Precious stones. 2. Minerals. 3. Precious stones—Washington (D.C.)—Catalogs.
    4. Minerals—Washington (D.C.)—Catalogs. 5. National Museum of Natural History (U.S.)—Catalogs.
    I. Post, Jeffrey Edward. II. Title.
    QE392.N38   1997
    553.8 ' 074 ' 753—dc21
                                                                       97–7633

Printed and bound in Japan

Harry N. Abrams, Inc.
100 Fifth Avenue
New York, N.Y. 10011
www.abramsbooks.com

CONTENTS

6

1. INTRODUCTION

GEMS AND MINERALS

Gemstones are among Earth's rarest and most beautiful creations. They have been called the flowers of the mineral kingdom, but unlike the ephemeral glory of a blossom, the beauty of a precious stone is undiminished with time. It is this that distinguishes gems from most other objects desired by people. Gems accumulate history. The very stone that once adorned a king or queen might today be set in someone's dinner ring and, if it is not destroyed, will still sparkle as brightly ten thousand years from now.

Since ancient times gems have been coveted because they are valuable, probably more so per volume than any other artifacts from or on the Earth. They are history's preeminent symbols of great wealth and tokens of power, used not only in objects of political significance but also as amulets, talismans, and charms. Their small size and consequent portability make them an important currency even today.

Gems are mineral crystals that have been cut and polished into objects of great beauty by skilled craftspeople. Minerals are solid, inorganic chemical compounds that form naturally within the Earth. Each mineral has a unique combination of chemical composition and atomic structure, which accounts for its hardness (defined as resistance to scratching), color, and other properties. There are approximately four thousand known minerals, and fifty to one hundred new ones are discovered each year. This diversity is the result of the many different combinations of temperature, pressure, and chemical elements that exist in the Earth. Some minerals are abundant; for example, quartz, feldspars, micas, and a handful of other minerals make up the bulk of the rocks in the Earth's crust. Other minerals form under such exotic conditions that they have been found in only one place in the world, or in a single hand specimen. Some of the important gem minerals, such as quartz, are common, and others are rare.

The formal definition specifies that minerals are inorganic, thereby excluding biological materials such as coral, ivory, pearls, and amber, even though some are chemically and structurally identical to certain minerals (pearls, for example, are primarily a calcium carbonate phase that is the same as the mineral aragonite). Nonetheless, many biological materials are popular in jewelry and traditionally have been included in gem collections and exhibitions.

Page 6:
This 15,256-carat (3.1 kg, or 6.8 lb) natural beryl (aquamarine) crystal is exceptional for its size and clarity. Its near perfect shape and few internal flaws indicate that it grew in ideal conditions. Large aquamarine crystals of this quality are rarely preserved; usually they are cut into gems. The 1,000-carat aquamarine gem, also from Brazil, is nicknamed "Most Precious" after a perfume created by its donor, Evyan Perfumes, Inc.

The Roebling Opal is an extraordinary 2,585-carat piece of opal rough from Virgin Valley, Nevada. The opal was deposited from silica-rich water in voids that remained after buried tree limbs had rotted away, in some cases resulting in opal casts of the original tree parts. Although extremely beautiful, opal from this locality is not commonly used in jewelry because it tends to craize, or crack. Gift of John A. Roebling, 1926

Minerals typically occur as crystals, meaning they are constructed of atoms linked together in a precise pattern that is repeated in an orderly way in three dimensions billions and billions of times. Most mineral crystals form from water solutions or magma (molten rock). Initially a few atoms cluster together, perhaps in response to slight changes in temperature or composition. This seed crystal grows as more and more atoms lock into place, methodically and precisely repeating the basic atomic arrangement. If many crystals are growing simultaneously in close proximity, they will crowd one another and not be able to grow very large or develop well-formed geometric shapes. This was the situation for most rocks, such as granite, that are made up of relatively small (less than one centimeter) crystals. Large, perfectly formed crystals need room to grow, such as in fissures and cavities and other openings in rocks, and they need ideal growing conditions: proper temperature, a steady supply of the right kind of atoms, and sufficient time (which can be thousands

or even millions of years). On the rare occasions that such ideal growing conditions are achieved in the Earth, the result can be spectacular crystals without flaws or other internal imperfections that are suitable for cutting into gems.

Any of the almost four thousand known minerals, if found as crystals of sufficient size and quality, could theoretically be cut into gems. In practice, however, only about fifteen mineral species account for most of the commercially available gems. A few hundred more have at one time or another also been cut into gems. Why are most minerals not popular as gems? Typically, they do not occur naturally as crystals that are large or clear enough to be cut into a gem, or, if suitable crystals have been found, they are too rare to be marketable. In other cases, the mineral might be too soft or brittle, or simply unattractive. Fashion and marketing strategies also influence the popularity of gem materials.

In most cases, the term *gem* refers to a mineral crystal that has been cut and polished. But there are some gem materials that are not cut from individual crystals; rather, they are compact masses composed of millions of tiny crystals (and are, therefore, technically rocks). They are generally opaque to translucent and are prized for their color and patterns, and for properties such as toughness that make them suitable for carving. Typically these materials are cut as cabochons and beads, or used for carving and a host of other decorative applications. Some of the most important of these fine-grained ornamental stones are jade, agate, lapis lazuli, turquoise, and malachite.

GEM CUTTING

The steady growth in the popularity of gems during the past several centuries has been due both to increased availability, as new sources were discovered and exploited, and to major advances in the gem cutter's art. Refinements in cutting and polishing methods along with a better understanding of the way light interacts with gemstones greatly improved the appearance of cut stones, and the demand for gems increased accordingly.

Gem cutting is an ancient art that has evolved from the fashioning of crude beads and carvings to the production of precisely cut faceted gems. Prior to about the seventeenth century, most gems were cut into rounded forms called cabochons, from an Old French word meaning "head." The concept of faceting

The great variety of cutting styles exhibited by these fluorite gems is a consequence of many factors, such as the size, shape, and depth of color of the original rough, the ultimate planned use of the gem, and the skill and whim of the gem cutter. Fluorite gems are popular for their great variety of candy-colored pastels, but they are too soft and fragile to be used in most jewelry. This selection includes gems from the United States, Switzerland, Spain, Korea, South Africa, Namibia, England, Colombia, and Tanzania, ranging in size from 24 to 900 carats

stones was likely inspired by the dazzling appearance of light reflecting off the naturally smooth, flat faces of certain mineral crystals. Faceting involves cutting and polishing flat faces in geometric patterns on the surface of the mineral to best show off the brilliance and color of the gemstone. Facets on older gemstones conform largely to their natural crystal faces, but with advances in cutting techniques faceting rapidly evolved into a sophisticated art.

The process of transforming a mineral crystal into a glittering gem varies for each kind of gemstone according to its particular properties, such as hardness, fragility, and optical characteristics. The basic steps, however, are similar. Before beginning the cutting process, the gem cutter carefully studies the rough crystal to locate the area that will produce the largest gem that is free from inclusions (tiny mineral grains or bubbles of gas or liquid trapped within the crystal) and other flaws. This process is commonly assisted today by computer-based 3-dimensional imaging techniques. The gem cutter must also ascertain how best to orient the stone so that the finished gem will show the most attractive color. Next the crystal is cut with a diamond saw or laser and shaped on an abrasive wheel. The facets are ground onto the stone at precisely determined angles. Finally the gem is polished on a wheel infused with a polishing agent. The extremely smooth surfaces produced by polishing enable light to be reflected more efficiently, increasing the gem's brilliance. Polishing also enhances the color of many gems by making it possible to see deeper into the gem. The quality of the cut can make the difference between a dazzling gem and a lifeless lump of mineral and is a significant factor when setting a gem's value.

Different cuts bring out special qualities of the various kinds of gemstones. The nonfaceted cabochon is best for displaying opaque and translucent stones and optical effects such as stars and cat's eyes. Virtually all faceted gems today are variations of the step or brilliant cuts. The step cut, or emerald cut, enhances the deep color of emeralds and other intensely colored gems. The round brilliant cut maximizes the reflectivity and fire, or dispersion, of diamonds and certain other gems. The marquise, oval, and pear shapes are variations of the brilliant cut.

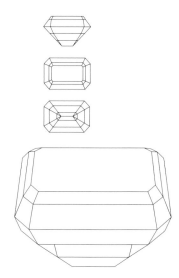

The emerald cut, or step cut (above), is designed to permit a maximum amount of light to enter the stone, bringing out the color of emeralds and other intensely colored gems. The brilliant cut (below) is associated primarily with diamonds. A brilliant-cut gem with the proper shape and proportions reflects most of the light entering it back out the top, thus maximizing its brilliance. As the light passes through a brilliant-cut diamond, its component colors are dispersed, giving the gem its fire

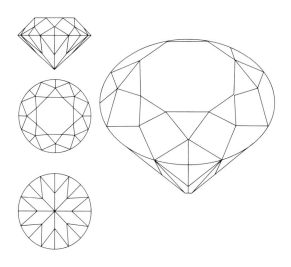

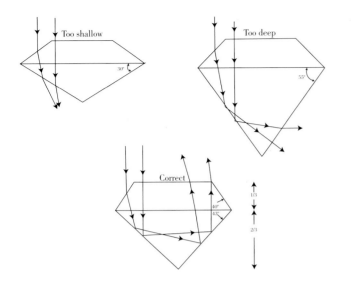

Diamonds must be cut with the proper angles and proportions in order to show their maximum brilliancy. Some of the light entering a gem that is cut either too shallow or deep will pass out the bottom or sides, reducing the brilliancy. In a properly cut stone all of the light is reflected off the inner surfaces of the facets and back out the top of the stone

Typically, gemstones are measured by their weight in carats. The metric carat is defined as 0.2 grams (.007 ounces), and each carat is divided into 100 points. The word *carat* comes from carob, a tree that grows in the Mediterranean region. For centuries carob seeds were used as a standard for weighing precious stones. The metric carat was adopted in the United States in 1913 and throughout the world by 1930. Prior to that time many different definitions of carat were used, making for considerable confusion in the gem trade. Because the density, or mass per unit volume, is not the same for all minerals, different gemstones having the same carat weight might not have the same volume. For example, the density of zircon (4.7 grams/cm^3) is considerably greater than that of diamond (3.5 grams/cm^3), and a one-carat diamond appears larger than a one-carat zircon.

THE COLORS OF GEMS

The most prized and recognizable trait of most gems is color, and, historically, stones with intense hues such as emeralds, rubies, and sapphires were most highly valued. Colorless stones, such as diamonds, have become fashionable only with the development of cutting styles that show off their brilliance and fire.

What gives minerals, and gems, their colors? The same process that gives any object its color—the way its atoms interact with visible light. White light is made up of a combination of the spectrum of colors. Some of these colors are absorbed by certain atoms in the crystal or gem and others pass through the crystal unaffected. The part of the light that is not absorbed is what we see as color. For example, if atoms in a gem absorb all of the red light, only the green-blue light will be transmitted to our eye, and the stone will appear green-blue. The various kinds of atoms and atomic arrangements in minerals absorb light differently, giving rise to an almost limitless range of colors. If all colors are absorbed, then the crystal or gem appears black, and if no light is absorbed it is colorless or white.

In order to understand in detail why gems, or any objects, have color, we must take a closer look at what happens when light encounters an atom.

Atoms have a nucleus of neutrons and protons surrounded by electrons in discrete energy levels. Light is a form of energy, and the different colors have different amounts of energy—violet is the most energetic and red is the least. If some color of light entering an atom has just the right amount of energy to kick an electron from its normal energy level to a higher one, that color of light will be used up, or absorbed, performing that task. The other colors of light pass through the atom unaffected. The newly promoted electron quickly falls back to its normal energy level, giving off the excess energy as a small amount of heat. This electron "aerobics" repeats over and over as long as light shines on the atom. The particular color of light that is absorbed by an atom depends

Many minerals occur in a variety of colors, depending upon the kinds of trace impurities they contain. These giant quartz gems include amethyst (purple), rose quartz (pink), citrine (gold-yellow), smoky quartz (gray-black), and rock crystal (colorless). They range in size from 375 carats to 2,670 carats and are all from Brazil. The light smoky gem (top) contains tiny hairlike, golden crystals of rutile

upon the energy differences between electron energy levels, which is a consequence of the kind of atom and the arrangement of the other atoms around it in a crystal. It is interesting to note that color is the result of a dynamic process, and that color is produced only as long as light is present. A red ruby, or your blue sweater, has no color in a dark room.

Fluorescence is another term encountered in discussions of gem colors. Fluorescence is a related phenomenon to that described above for color, but is triggered by ultraviolet light, which is invisible and more energetic than visible light. The sun's ultraviolet rays cause sunburn, while a less potent variety is emitted by the so-called black lights popular in some discotheques. Ultraviolet light also can boost electrons into higher energy levels, but in this case when the electrons fall back to their original levels they give off their newly acquired energy as visible light, the color of which depends upon the amount of excess energy. Fluorescence is best observed in a dark room, but in some cases it is bright enough that it is apparent even under normal lighting conditions; for example, the brilliant red of a Burmese ruby is enhanced by a deep red fluorescence. If, instead of falling back to its normal energy level immediately, an excited electron remains at its higher energy state for some period of time, then light might be given off by a specimen for seconds or even minutes after the ultraviolet light has been removed, a phenomenon called phosphorescence.

Some minerals are always the same color. Malachite, for example, is always green, due to the presence of copper. The copper atoms absorb all colors of light entering the stone except for green. Many minerals, including most of the important gem minerals, such as corundum, beryl, and quartz, are colorless if chemically pure, and it is the presence of impurities and defects in their atomic structures that is responsible for the vivid hues they sometimes exhibit. For example, the addition of a few chromium atoms turns normally colorless corundum to vivid red ruby, since the chromium atoms absorb all colors of light except red. If the impurity atoms in corundum are iron and titanium, deep blue sapphires result. Likewise, the mineral beryl occurs in a wide range of colors, depending on which kinds of impurity atoms were incorporated by the growing crystals. Chromium atoms are responsible for the deep green variety of beryl known as emerald, and iron provides aquamarine's delicate shades. It may seem curious that while chromium atoms give ruby its deep red color, they are also responsible for emerald's vivid green hue. In the two different minerals (corundum and beryl, respectively) the chromium atoms are surrounded by different arrangements of oxygen atoms, which affect the positions of their electron energy levels. Consequently, the energy, and color, of light absorbed is different.

The National Gem Collection

When Englishman James Smithson left his fortune in 1829 to the then fledgling United States of America for the establishment of the Smithsonian Institution, he also bequeathed his collection of more than ten thousand mineral specimens. Smithson was a chemist and mineralogist, and the zinc carbonate mineral smithsonite, which he first described as a distinct mineral, was named after him. Unfortunately his complete collection and its documentation were destroyed in a devastating fire in the Smithsonian Castle Building in 1865. It is not known whether Smithson's collection included cut gems, but almost certainly there were minerals that are commonly used as gems.

The present National Gem Collection at the Smithsonian Institution started in 1884 when Professor Frank W. Clarke, chief chemist at the United States Geological Survey and honorary curator in the Division of Mineralogy, assembled a modest collection of American precious stones that were displayed as part of the National Museum's contribution to the New Orleans's Exhibition of that year. Using $2,500 appropriated by the Commission for the Exhibition, he acquired a thousand specimens (an average of only $2.50 per specimen), about one-third of which were cut and polished. The collection was displayed at the Cincinnati Exhibition the following year and then returned to the National Museum, where the gems were arranged in two flat, plate-glass exhibition cases. In 1886 the noted gemologist George F. Kunz described the collection as a much needed accession and stated, "Although a mere beginning, it is the most complete public collection of gems in the United States." In 1891, the museum purchased, for $500, a collection of 150 gems (the price had increased to $3.33 per stone) from the estate of the naturalist Dr. Joseph Leidy of Philadelphia. These were combined with the existing gems to form an exhibit for the World's Columbian Exposition at Chicago in 1893.

The collection received a major boost in 1894 with the bequest of 1,316 precious stones from Dr. Isaac Lea's extensive collection by his daughter, Mrs. Frances Lea Chamberlain. This was followed in 1896 by a notable gift of

In the 1920s, the gem exhibit at the National Museum of Natural History consisted of a row of table cases extending down the center of the mineral hall

gems, chiefly from the United States, from Mrs. Chamberlain's husband, Dr. Leander T. Chamberlain. In 1897, Dr. Chamberlain became honorary curator of the collection and added several fine gems and later bequeathed a modest endowment for gem acquisition.

In 1910, the gem collection moved from the Arts and Industries Building to the new National Museum of Natural History, and during the period 1917–19 the gem collection was recatalogued and separated from the mineral collection. By 1922, the gem exhibit consisted of a row of table cases extending down the center of the mineral hall. George P. Merrill, the curator at the time, described the gem collection as "poorly balanced, lacking a satisfactory showing of the rarer and highly priced stones." He also indicated that the great popularity of the gem collection impressed upon the museum authorities the advisability of extending the collection, but progress was slow because of the expense involved.

The next significant event in the growth of the gem collection was the acquisition, in 1926, of the superb mineral collection of Colonel Washington A. Roebling, presented by his son, John A. Roebling. Colonel Roebling is probably best known to most people as the builder of the Brooklyn Bridge. The Roebling gift represented seventy years of active collecting and included many fine rough and cut gems. During the same year the museum also received the Fredrick A. Canfield collection, which, although it did not include any important gems, contained many gem-quality crystals. Both collections were accompanied by modest endowments, which continue to support the collection.

Undoubtedly the single most important event that established the worldwide reputation of the National Gem Collection was the gift, on November 10, 1958, by Harry Winston of the renowned Hope Diamond. The gift coincided with the opening of the newly renovated mineral hall and gem room. In addition to the Hope Diamond, the new gem display consisted of more than a

Left:
Dr. Isaac Lea (1792–1880) assembled a superb gem collection. In 1894, his daughter, Mrs. Frances Lea Chamberlain, donated 1,316 gems to the Smithsonian Institution

Right:
In 1926, Frederick A. Canfield (1849–1926), a mining engineer, donated a collection of nine thousand specimens that was particularly rich in minerals from New Jersey's renowned zinc mines

thousand individual stones. This exhibition served many tens of millions visitors until it was closed for renovation in 1995.

The addition of the Hope Diamond triggered a series of major gifts from generous individuals. These included the Blue Heart Diamond, the Napoleon Necklace and Diadem, and the Maximilian Emerald from Mrs. Marjorie Merriweather Post, the Logan Sapphire from Mrs. John Logan, the Victoria-Transvaal Diamond from Victoria and Leonard Wilkinson, a large emerald and suite of yellow diamonds from Janet Annenberg Hooker, and the spectacular star ruby from Mr. Rosser Reeves, among many others, that have built the National Gem Collection into the greatest public display of gemstones in the world. One of the notable aspects of this collection is that it has come about almost entirely because of the generosity of private individuals. While the major emphasis for acquisitions for the National Gem Collection has always been on gems rather than jewelry, over the years several important jewelry pieces have been added. In some cases they contain significant gems, but in others they have been acquired primarily because of their historical interest. Jewelry represents the joint craftmanship of nature and people, and historical jewels further intrigue us by providing a link to the past.

Today the National Gem Collection consists of more than ten thousand

Left:
Washington A. Roebling (1837–1926), the engineer who designed New York City's Brooklyn Bridge, possessed one of the finest private mineral collections of his time. In 1926, his son, John A. Roebling, donated 16,000 specimens to the Smithsonian Institution

Right:
In 1958, renowned jeweler Harry Winston (1898–1978) donated the Hope Diamond to the Smithsonian Institution, sparking a new period of intense interest and growth in the National Gem Collection

gems and jewelry pieces and continues to grow. All of the most important pieces are displayed in the Janet Annenberg Hooker Hall of Geology, Gems and Minerals, the museum's completely renovated exhibitions of gems, minerals, and earth science that opened in 1997. In a major departure from the previous hall, most of the gems are displayed alongside the corresponding natural crystals. The remaining gems form a reference collection used by researchers in gemology, mineralogy, and material science. In many cases, because gems are cut from the most perfect crystals, they are the preferred, and required, samples for certain kinds of scientific studies, for example, spectroscopy and crystallographic measurements.

2. Historical Jewels in the Collection

THE HOPE DIAMOND

The world-famous Hope Diamond is viewed by more than six million visitors annually, making it the most sought-out object in the entire Smithsonian Institution and perhaps in any museum in the world. Ironically, only a small percentage of those visitors know anything about the Hope Diamond or why it is famous. Many expect to see the world's largest diamond, which, at 45.52 carats, the Hope certainly is not. (The largest cut diamond is the golden Jubilee owned by the King of Thailand; at 545.67 carats, it is more than ten times the size of the Hope Diamond.) Most people are surprised to see that it is a colored stone and does not even look like a diamond. So why is the Hope Diamond so famous? First, it is the largest

Page 20:
The Hope Diamond is currently in a platinum setting, surrounded by sixteen white pear-shaped and cushion-cut diamonds, suspended from a chain containing forty-five diamonds, designed by Pierre Cartier in about 1910. Gift of Harry Winston, 1958

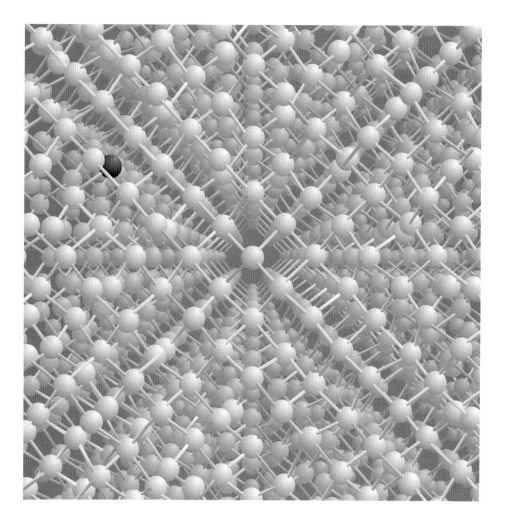

Left:
Diamond is hard because each of its carbon atoms is strongly linked to four other carbon atoms. The blue color of the Hope Diamond is caused by light interacting with boron atoms (depicted as black in this diagram), substituting for about one out of every million carbon atoms

known deep blue diamond; only about one in one hundred thousand diamonds is sufficiently colored to be called a fancy-colored diamond, and of these blue is one of the rarest and most desirable hues. Deep blue diamonds larger than a few carats are exceedingly rare. Therefore, the Hope Diamond is special because it is a unique natural object. But undoubtedly the major reason why the Hope Diamond is one of the world's most famous gems is its more than three-century history of mystery and intrigue, one that includes kings, a revolution, a daring theft, and perhaps even a curse.

The period of time since the Hope Diamond's discovery by humans in India, however, is just the most recent chapter in an epic adventure that started more than a billion years ago. Based on studies of many diamonds and of the diamond deposits in India, it is possible to formulate a likely early history of the gem we now know as the Hope Diamond. Most diamonds that have been dated by scientists are between one and three billion years old. (The Hope Diamond does not contain the inclusions of other mineral crystals that are necessary for age measurements, and even if it did, the destructive nature of the measurement would preclude such a study.) Studies show that diamonds form more than 150 km (93 mi) below the Earth's surface, in the upper mantle, where temperatures reach 1,200 °C (2,192 °F). Intense pressure from the weight of the overlying rock compresses carbon atoms into the compact arrangement of diamond. In the case of the Hope Diamond, a small number of boron atoms substituted for some of the carbon atoms (approximately one per million), giving rise to the blue color.

After being underground for millions, or even billions, of years, the diamond was carried to the Earth's surface by a volcanic eruption in just a few hours. During this wild ride the diamond was in great jeopardy. It could have shattered during the upward journey or the explosive surface eruption. Or, if the trip to the surface had been too slow, the diamond might have altered to graphite, the soft ingredient in pencils and the more stable form of carbon at the low temperatures and pressures near the Earth's surface. As the magma carrying the diamond approached the surface at speeds of up to 70 km (43 mi) per hour, gases in the magma bubbled out. The magma turned to foam and erupted explosively, as when a warm bottle of soda is opened. At the surface the magma hardened into a type of rock called kimberlite, within which was entombed the diamond. Age measurements on rocks from the diamond deposits in India where the Hope Diamond was found indicate that the diamond probably arrived at the Earth's surface about a billion years ago. Water and wind gradually eroded the kimberlite, freeing the diamond, which was incorporated into the resulting gravel deposits.

It is not known exactly when and where the Hope Diamond was discovered, but it was prior to 1668 and most likely in the Golconda area of India. This region was the only major source of diamonds in the world prior to their discovery in Brazil in 1723. The Kollur mine, in particular, was well known as a source of colored diamonds. In 1668, Jean-Baptiste Tavernier, a French gem merchant, sold a 112 3/16-carat (approximately 110.5 metric carats) blue diamond from India to King Louis XIV of France. The diamond was cut in the Indian style, which emphasized size rather than brilliance; probably only the natural crystal faces were polished. The king had the stone recut to a heart shape in 1673, improving its brilliance and reducing it to 67 1/8 carats (69.03 metric carats). It is unlikely that any small diamonds could have been fashioned from the cuttings of the original stone. In 1749 Louis XV had the diamond, now known as the French Blue, set into a piece of ceremonial jewelry for the Order of the Golden Fleece, which also featured a large white diamond and a red spinel, and was worn only by the king. During the reign of King Louis XVI and Queen Marie-Antoinette the French Revolution erupted, and sometime between September 11 and September 17, 1792, the royal treasury was looted and the Crown Jewels, including the French Blue, disappeared.

The whereabouts of the stolen blue diamond for the next twenty years remains a mystery. Finally, in 1812, a memorandum by John Francillon, a London jeweler, dated precisely twenty years and two days after the French Crown Jewels had been reported missing, documented the presence of a 44 1/4-carat (45.5 modern metric carats) blue diamond in England in the possession of London diamond merchant Daniel Eliason. This diamond was undoubtedly cut from the French Blue, a contention supported by the fact that, according to French law, the statute of limitations for any crimes committed during wartime was twenty years, of which Francillon and his client were surely aware. The Francillon memorandum established the person in possession of the diamond as its new legal owner.

For the next several years it is not known what happened to the diamond,

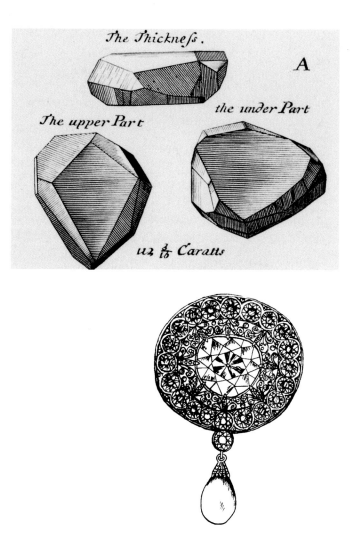

Jean-Baptiste Tavernier (opposite) was the French gem merchant who, in 1668, sold King Louis XIV a large blue diamond from which the Hope Diamond was eventually cut. The drawing by Tavernier below shows three views of his 112 3/16-carat blue diamond. It was crudely cut, and Tavernier described the color as a beautiful violet

Lord Henry Philip Hope (opposite) was a banker and collector of fine gems. In a catalogue of his collection published in 1839, the diamond that now bears his name was described as a fine, deep sapphire blue and was set in a medallion with a border of small rose-cut diamonds, surrounded by a border of twenty brilliant-cut diamonds (above)

Right:

A memorandum by John Francillon, dated September 19, 1812, documents a 44¼-carat (45.5 metric carat) deep blue diamond in the possession of London diamond merchant Daniel Eliason. Francillon's sketches of the top and side views of the diamond match those of the Hope Diamond

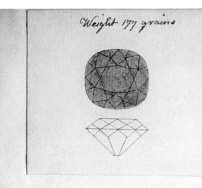

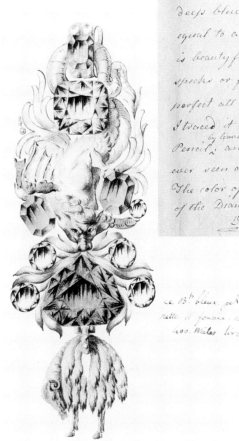

Left:

In 1749, King Louis XV had the 67⅛-carat French Blue diamond set in a ceremonial piece of jewelry for the Order of the Golden Fleece. The piece also featured the Côte de Bretagne, a 105-carat red spinel carved in the shape of a dragon, and a large white diamond. The illustration is based on a lead model made of the original jewelry piece

but there is some evidence to suggest that around 1820 it was bought by King George IV. The gem historian John Mawe states in his book *A Treatise on Diamonds and Precious Stones* (1823) that, "A superlatively fine blue diamond weighing 44 carats, and valued at 30,000 pounds, formerly the property of our Mr. Eliason, an eminent diamond merchant, is now said to be in the possession of our most gracious sovereign." Sometime after George IV's death in 1830, the diamond was purchased by a London banker and gem collector, Henry Philip Hope, whose name it bears today. After Hope's death in 1839, the diamond was left to his nephew Henry Thomas Hope, who then left it to his grandson Lord Francis Hope. In 1901, Lord Hope sold it to Adolph Weil, a London dealer, to pay off his debts. It was quickly sold to Joseph Frankels & Sons of New York and then to Selim Habib, who put it up for auction in Paris in 1909. It did not sell at auction, but was sold soon after to C. H. Rosenau and then to Pierre Cartier in the same year.

Evalyn Walsh McLean first saw the Hope Diamond while visiting Paris in 1910. Her father had struck it rich mining gold in Colorado, which allowed her to indulge her taste for extravagant jewels. Nevertheless, the mounting of the gem did not appeal to her and she returned to her home in Washington, D.C., without it. Pierre Cartier, however, was not one to give up easily; a few months later, diamond in hand, in a new setting, he arrived at McLean's home and left it with her for the weekend. His sales strategy was apparently successful, and over the next several months the deal was negotiated to purchase the diamond for $180,000. Cartier told Mrs. McLean that the diamond brought bad luck to anyone who wore it, but this was likely no more than a sales pitch, since she had told him that she felt objects that were bad luck for others were good luck for her. It seems that subsequent stories about the Hope Diamond being cursed or causing ill fortune stem from Cartier's attempts to interest Mrs. McLean in the diamond. If he did not completely fabricate these stories, he certainly embellished them.

Mrs. McLean added greatly to the legend of the Hope Diamond. She wore it everywhere and loved to tell stories about it. She entertained frequently, and many people had the opportunity to try on or hold the diamond. According to one account it was even modeled by her Great Dane, Mike. She pawned the diamond several times when she needed ready cash and offered it to help pay the ransom when the nation was in the grip of the drama of the kidnapping of Charles and Anne Morrow Lindbergh's baby boy in 1932. Two years after her death in 1947, her entire collection of jewelry, including the Hope Diamond, was purchased by the prominent New York jeweler Harry Winston. For the next nine years the diamond traveled the country as part of Winston's fabulous "Court of Jewels" exhibit. In 1958, the diamond was removed from its setting and the culet (bottom) facet was slightly recut.

Above:
Evalyn Walsh McLean wearing the Hope Diamond, suspended from which are two other large diamonds, the 94.8-carat Star of the East and the 31.26-carat McLean Diamond

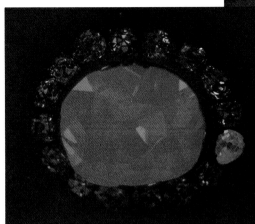

The Hope Diamond (right) weighs 45.52 carats and measures 25.60 x 21.78 x 12.00 mm. It is an asymmetrical cushion antique brilliant with 58 facets plus two extra facets on the pavilion and additional facets on the girdle. It was described by the Gemological Institute of America in 1996 as an intense fancy, dark grayish blue with VS_1-VVS_1 clarity. (The stone shows some whitish graining and surface wear marks.) The highly unusual intense orange-red phosphorescence (above) of the diamond is only visible in a dark room after exposure to ultraviolet light. Orange-red phosphorescence is almost exclusively limited to dark blue diamonds, but seldom with the intensity exhibited by the Hope Diamond. The photograph also shows one of the diamonds surrounding the Hope Diamond phosphorescing blue

The Hope Diamond
actual size

On November 10, 1958, the Hope Diamond was presented by Mr. Winston to the Smithsonian Institution as the foundation of a great National Gem Collection. It arrived in a plain brown package by registered mail—insured for one million dollars. With only a few brief exceptions the diamond has remained on continuous exhibition at the National Museum of Natural History. Since the arrival of the Hope Diamond, the National Gem Collection has grown steadily in size and stature, and is today considered by many to be the finest public display of gems in the world. For the Smithsonian Institution, the Hope Diamond obviously has been a source of good luck.

THE NAPOLEON DIAMOND NECKLACE

This elegant diamond necklace was a gift from Emperor Napoleon I to his second wife, Marie-Louise, in celebration of the birth of their son, the emperor of Rome, in 1811. The necklace was designed and assembled by the prominent jewelry firm Etienne Nitôt et Fils of Paris and completed in June 1811 for the fee of 376,274 francs. It is constructed of twenty-eight oval and cushion-cut diamonds, suspending a fringe of nineteen briolette-cut oval and pear-shaped diamonds, and accented by small, round diamonds and diamond-set motifs. The setting is silver and gold, and the estimated total weight of the diamonds is 263 carats. The largest weighs approximately 10 carats.

Following the fall of Napoleon, Marie-Louise returned in 1814 to her Hapsburg family in Vienna, taking all of her jewelry, including this necklace. After her death in 1847, the necklace passed to Archduchess Sophie of Austria, her sister-in-law and the mother of Emperor Franz Joseph. The archduchess removed two stones (about 2.5 carats each) to shorten the necklace and had earrings made from them, the whereabouts of which are unknown. Archduchess Sophie wore the necklace at the coronation ceremonies of Alexander III of Russia, and apparently it was so admired that it was put on display for the court ladies. The necklace was bequeathed in 1872 to Archduchess Sophie's third son, Archduke Karl Ludwig of Austria. In 1929, Archduchess Maria Therese sent the necklace to New York to be sold, only to fall prey to an unscrupulous merchant who priced it way below market value and returned only $16,000 to the archduchess, absconding with the rest of the money. The scandal that ensued precipitated several arrests and lawsuits, and eventually the necklace was returned to the archduchess. The necklace remained in the Hapsburg family until 1948, when Ludwig's grandson, Prince Franz Joseph of Liechtenstein, sold it to a French collector, who in turn sold it to Harry Winston in 1960. Marjorie Merriweather Post acquired the necklace from Winston and presented it to the Smithsonian Institution in 1962.

The diamonds in the Napoleon Necklace came from India and/or Brazil, the only significant diamond-producing areas in the world at that time. They are cut in the "old mine" style, a precursor to the modern brilliant cut. This cutting style yields stones with dazzling dispersion—flashes of color as the stones move in the light—but they lack the brilliance of modern stones cut to

Empress Marie-Louise wearing the diamond necklace that is now in the National Gem Collection

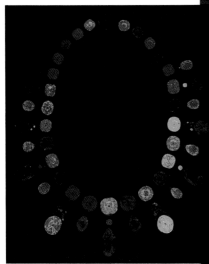

The Napoleon Necklace (right) was presented by Napoleon I to Empress Marie-Louise in celebration of the birth of their son in 1811. The total weight of diamonds is approximately 263 carats; the largest is about 10.5 carats. Under ultraviolet light in a dark room (above), many of the diamonds in the necklace glow brightly in hues of blue, yellow, and orange. Fluorescence is exhibited by about one-fifth of all diamonds and results from the interaction of the ultraviolet light with trace chemical impurities in the stones. The pattern of fluorescent diamonds can be useful for documenting and authenticating certain jewelry pieces. Gift of Mrs. Marjorie Merriweather Post, 1962

exacting proportions to ensure maximum reflection of light through the top of the stone. Light passing out the bottom of the stone in old mine-cut diamonds reduces the overall brilliance and causes the dark bowtie-shaped "windows" visible in the centers of many of the diamonds in the Napoleon Necklace.

The diamond and silver Marie-Louise Diadem was a wedding
gift from Napoleon I to his second wife, Empress Marie-Louise.
The original emeralds were replaced by Persian turquoise in
1954–62. Gift of Mrs. Marjorie Merriweather Post, 1971

It is perhaps surprising to see turquoise in this magnificent diadem, another gift (probably on the occasion of their marriage) of Napoleon to Marie-Louise. In fact, originally the diadem, commissioned in 1810, was set with emeralds, which were replaced in this century with turquoise. It too was made by Etienne Nitôt et Fils of Paris. The diadem was one piece of a parure that also included a necklace, comb, belt buckle, and earrings, all in emeralds, diamonds, silver, and gold. The necklace, currently owned by the jewelry firm Van Cleef & Arpels, still has its emeralds; the emeralds have been removed from the comb. The whereabouts of the earrings and belt buckle are unknown. The diadem is an elaborate design of scrolls, palmettes, and medallions and currently contains 79 Persian turquoise stones (540 carats) and 1,006 mine-cut diamonds (totaling approximately 700 carats), set in silver and gold.

Marie-Louise bequeathed the diadem and accompanying jewelry to her Hapsburg aunt, Archduchess Elise. The jewelry was acquired by Van Cleef & Arpels from one of Archduchess Elise's descendants, Archduke Karl Stefan Hapsburg of Sweden, in 1953, along with a document attesting to their provenance. The pieces were in a saddle-shaped jewelry case.

During the period from May 1954 through June 1956, the emeralds were removed from the diadem by Van Cleef & Arpels and sold individually in pieces of jewelry. A newspaper advertisement placed by the company in 1955 promised: "An emerald for you from the historic Napoleonic Tiara. . . ." Sometime between 1956 and 1962, Van Cleef & Arpels mounted the turquoise into the diadem. In 1962, the diadem, with turquoise, was displayed in the Louvre in Paris along with the necklace, earrings, and comb, as part of a special exhibition on Marie-Louise. Marjorie Merriweather Post purchased the diadem from Van Cleef & Arpels for the Smithsonian Institution in 1971.

The diadem with the original emeralds

Marjorie Merriweather Post (1887–1973) wearing the Marie-Louise Diadem. Mrs. Post was heiress to the Post cereal fortune and a collector of French and Russian art. The diadem is one of several major donations she made to the National Gem Collection

THE MARIE-ANTOINETTE EARRINGS

According to tradition, more than two hundred years ago the diamonds in these earrings were among the favorite pieces of jewelry of Queen Marie-Antoinette of France (1755–1793; queen: 1774–1792). In his history of the French Crown Jewels, Germain Bapst states that King Louis XVI, at the beginning of his reign, gave Marie-Antoinette a pair of earrings with large pear-shaped diamonds hanging from four other diamonds at the posts in a silver and gold setting. He also reports that she wore them constantly. It is possible that the stones had been part of a suite of large pear-shaped diamonds assembled for Madam Jeanne du Barry, consort of King Louis XV. Like the Hope Diamond, the earrings disappeared in the chaos of the French Revolution, although being the queen's personal property, they were not among the Crown Jewels that were stolen in September 1792.

When jeweler Pierre Cartier purchased the diamond earrings in 1928, their authenticity was attested to in an affidavit by Russian Princess Zenaide Youssoupoff and her son, Prince Felix Youssoupoff, stating that they originally belonged to Queen Marie-Antoinette and had never been reset in the one hundred years that they were in their family. They claimed to have acquired the earrings by direct inheritance from the Grand Duchess Tatiana Youssoupoff (1769–1841). The story passed down through their family relates that the earrings were with Queen Marie-Antoinette during the royal family's attempt to flee Paris in June 1791, and that they were taken from her when the entourage was stopped at Varennes and sent back to the capital as prisoners of the Revolution. It is not known how the earrings came into the possession of the grand duchess, although according to a 1905 biography by Grand Duke Nicholas, she had a passion for precious stones and bought them throughout Europe. He also states that she had the means to assemble a great collection, which included, among other significant jewels, the earrings of Marie-Antoinette.

Another version of the earrings' disappearance appears in the memoirs of Mme. Jeanne Louise Genêt Campan, Marie Antoinette's lady-in-waiting, who relates that while most of the queen's personal jewelry had been sent to Brussels for safekeeping at the beginning of the time of troubles, the diamond earrings, described as composed of a ring or band and two pear-shaped

The Marie-Antoinette diamonds, 20.34 and 14.25 carats, respectively, are set in diamond and platinum settings by Harry Winston, Inc., that are replicas of the originals. The diamond and platinum tops were designed by Cartier Inc. Gift of Mrs. Eleanor Barzin, 1964

Queen Marie-
Antoinette

diamonds, remained in a bureau in the queen's room and were certainly seized when the mob stormed the Tuileries on August 10, 1792. While the circumstances by which Marie-Antoinette's diamond earrings left her possession may never be known with certainty, it seems plausible that sometime in the early nineteenth century they were acquired by Grand Duchess Tatiana of Russia.

In October of 1928 Pierre Cartier sold the Marie-Antoinette earrings to Marjorie Merriweather Post. At the time of the sale, Cartier described the settings as original, but it is not known if these had been replaced or altered in the previous century. The large diamond drops were surrounded by bands of silver that had gold linkages and were decorated with old mine-cut diamonds in scrollwork. Later, Cartier replaced the tops of the earrings with triangular diamonds set in platinum. In 1959, Harry Winston, Inc., mounted the diamonds into platinum and diamond replicas of the original drop settings. The drops were also made detachable and round diamonds and diamond-set links were added. Mrs. Post sometimes wore the diamond drops attached to a necklace with a 13.95-carat triangular diamond center. In November 1964, Mrs. Post's daughter, Mrs. Eleanor Barzin, donated the earrings, along with the original settings, to the Smithsonian Institution. The diamonds and links added to the drops by Winston's were removed prior to their donation, but they retain the Cartier tops and the modern platinum and diamond settings.

The large shallow, pear-shaped diamonds were recently removed from their settings and their weights determined to be 20.34 and 14.25 carats. The larger stone shows a strong pink-orange fluorescence under ultraviolet light. The diamonds are originally from India or Brazil, the only significant sources of diamonds in the eighteenth century.

The Spanish Inquisition Necklace

The large diamonds and emeralds in this elegant necklace were probably cut in India in the seventeenth century, making them the earliest fashioned gems in the National Gem Collection. According to legend, at least a portion, or variation, of this necklace was once the property of Spanish royalty and later adorned ladies of the French court. Unfortunately, information concerning the details of the early history of the necklace is extremely meager. It was apparently purchased early in the twentieth century by the maharaja of Indore. In 1948, Harry Winston acquired the necklace in its present form from the maharaja's son, and it became part of Winston's "Court of Jewels" traveling exhibition. In 1955, Harry Winston sold the necklace to Mrs. Cora Hubbard Williams of Pittsburgh, Pennsylvania. The Smithsonian Institution received the Spanish Inquisition Necklace as a bequest from Mrs. Williams in 1972.

The necklace is composed of two strands of antique-cut diamonds and emeralds to which a lower pendant and upper chain containing modern, brilliant-cut diamonds have been added. There is a total of 374 diamonds and 15 superb emeralds. All of the emeralds in the necklace undoubtedly came from Colombia. By the seventeenth century Spanish conquistadores were shipping large quantities of emeralds from the Chivor and Muzo mines in Colombia back to Europe. A large quantity of these emeralds was sent to India, where they were cut and polished. Subsequently, many of the finished gems and jewelry pieces were traded or sold back to European royalty. The sixteen pear-shaped diamonds are slightly yellowish in color and almost certainly came from India, the world's only significant source of diamonds prior to their discovery in Brazil in 1723.

The large, central, barrel-shaped emerald weighs approximately 45 carats, and its rich, velvety color and exceptional clarity place it among the world's very finest quality emeralds. The shape closely approximates the form of the original elongated, hexagonal crystal, suggesting that the crystal faces were simply rounded off in order to yield the largest possible gem. The emerald is strung onto the necklace through a hole drilled lengthwise down its center. It is remarkable that the inside of the hole was polished so as to make it less obvious.

The remaining barrel-shaped emeralds and sixteen large diamonds on the two central strands are also attached in a most extraordinary way. Each has two angled drill holes on one side that connect within the stone. A wire passing through the resulting V-shaped channel almost invisibly secures the stone to the necklace.

The origin of the name, Spanish Inquisition Necklace, remains a mystery. It seems likely, however, that the title was conferred in this century, in recognition of the connection of many of its gems to that epic period in Spain's history.

The large diamonds and emeralds in the Spanish Inquisition Necklace (right) were fashioned in India in the seventeenth century. The large central emerald weighs approximately 45 carats. The detail above shows the unusual method used to attach some of the gems to the necklace. Gift of Mrs. Cora Hubbard Williams, 1972

THE PORTUGUESE DIAMOND

The Portuguese Diamond at 127.01 carats is the largest faceted diamond in the National Gem Collection. Its near flawless clarity and unusual octagonal emerald cut make it one of the world's most magnificent diamond gems. It is perhaps more than a little surprising, then, that so little documented information exists about its origin and early history. The lack of an authoritative provenance, however, has given rise to considerable conjecture and legend. The diamond owes its current name to one such legend, according to which the diamond was found in Brazil in the mid-eighteenth century and became part of the Portuguese Crown Jewels. There is no documentation, however, that substantiates a Brazilian origin or connection to Portuguese royalty, nor is it clear where or from whom this story originated. As is discussed below, the diamond most likely was found at the Premier mine in Kimberley, South Africa, early in the twentieth century

Interestingly, the extensive media coverage that followed exhibitions of the diamond around the country during 1946–47 made no reference to the diamond by its current name or to a Portuguese or Brazilian connection. Instead other, sometimes conflicting, versions of the history of the diamond were presented. Most accounts indicate that the diamond, which was owned at the time by a syndicate of American diamond dealers, had mysteriously appeared in Amsterdam some years earlier as a rough cut, cushion-shaped stone weighing 187 carats, which was recut into its present form. They also state that diamond dealers all over the world were puzzled by the diamond's lack of history and had tried to trace its origin without success. One article, on the other hand, indicated that the diamond originally belonged to an Indian potentate who had pawned it in London. During this period when the diamond was exhibited at jewelry stores across the country it was suspended as a pendant from a platinum band set with 380 small diamonds.

One part of the diamond's history that is well documented is that in February 1928 Peggy Hopkins Joyce acquired the diamond from Black, Starr & Frost. She traded a $350,000 pearl necklace for the diamond and $23,000 in cash. According to New York newspaper accounts, it was mounted on a diamond-studded platinum choker to be worn close around the throat (probably the same necklace described above). The jewelry firm's spokesperson at the time indicated that the diamond was found at the Premier mine, Kimberley, South Africa, in

Peggy Hopkins Joyce wearing the Portuguese Diamond, which she acquired in 1928, set in a platinum and diamond necklace

1910, and that the firm had obtained it shortly after its discovery. Miss Joyce was a dazzling blonde who performed in the Ziegfeld Follies, a true glamour girl of the 1920s. She had six husbands, at least five of whom were men of wealth, and claimed to have been engaged fifty times. She was said to be almost as fond of jewels as of

The octagonal-shaped 127.01-carat Portuguese Diamond (right) is the largest cut diamond in the National Gem Collection. The apparent cloudiness in the stone is actually blue fluorescence that is so intense it shows up even under incandescent lights. When exposed to ultraviolet light, the Portuguese Diamond fluoresces bright blue, and is literally bright enough to read by (above)

men. Sometime prior to 1946 Miss Joyce placed the diamond on consignment to the group of jewelers mentioned above, in an unsuccessful attempt to sell it.

Harry Winston acquired the Portuguese Diamond from Miss Joyce in 1951, and for the next several years it traveled around the country as part of his "Court of Jewels" exhibition. In 1957, Winston sold the diamond to an international industrialist, who then traded it back in 1962. In 1963, the Smithsonian acquired the Portuguese Diamond from Mr. Winston in exchange for 2,400 carats of small diamonds.

The Portuguese Diamond strongly fluoresces blue under ultraviolet light. A soft fluorescence is visible even in daylight or artificial light and gives the stone a slight bluish haze, enough so that it was once advertised as the "largest blue diamond in the world." In fact, if not for the fluorescence, the diamond would appear slightly yellowish.

THE HOOKER EMERALD

This superb 75.47-carat emerald was once the property of Abdul Hamid II, sultan of the Ottoman Empire from 1876 until 1909. It is alleged that he wore it in his belt buckle. The emerald was acquired by Tiffany & Company prior to World War I. At the 1940 New York World's Fair "House of Jewels" exhibit, the emerald was set with 901 diamonds in a tiara, which included five detachable emerald brooches. By 1950 the emerald had been placed in the current brooch setting, and with matching earclips was featured on the first page of the Tiffany Christmas catalogue. Mrs. Janet Annenberg Hooker purchased the brooch from Tiffany & Company in 1955, and in 1977 she donated it to the Smithsonian Institution.

The Hooker Emerald is cut in an elegant beveled square, measuring 27 mm (1.06 in) on each edge. The stone originated from the famous mines of Colombia and probably was shipped to Europe by Spanish conquistadores in the sixteenth or seventeenth century. The gem exhibits exceptional color and is remarkably free from flaws and inclusions for an emerald of its size. In its current platinum brooch setting the emerald is surrounded by 109 round and 20 baguette diamonds, weighing a total of 13 carats.

Abdul Hamid II (1842–1918), who was said to wear the emerald in his belt buckle

In 1940, the Hooker Emerald was mounted in a tiara designed by Tiffany & Company

The 75.47-carat Hooker Emerald exhibits exceptional color and is remarkably free from flaws for an emerald of its size. Gift of Mrs. Janet Annenberg Hooker, 1977

The Tiffany & Company 1950 Christmas catalogue featured the Hooker Emerald

A diamond crystal (approximately 3 carats) embedded in an unusual volcanic rock called kimberlite. Kimberlite is composed largely of altered olivine and named for Kimberley, South Africa, where it was first studied. This specimen is from the Premier mine in South Africa

3. Diamond, Corundum, and Beryl

DIAMOND

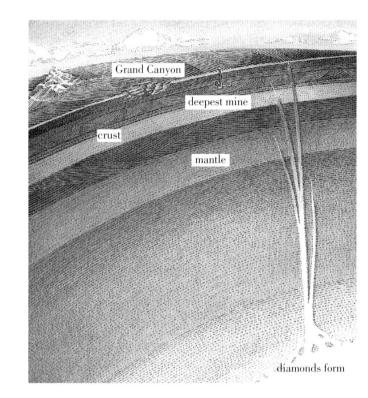

Diamonds form about 150 km (93 mi) beneath the Earth's surface and are propelled upward by explosive volcanic eruptions

Diamonds, like soot, are made of carbon. But diamonds form more than 150 km (93 mi) below the surface of the Earth, where temperatures exceed 1,200 °C (2,192 °F) and the intense pressure from the weight of the overlying rock compresses carbon atoms into a compact and exceptionally strong crystal structure. The list of superlatives on the diamond résumé propels it to the head of the gemstone class. It is the hardest substance known. (The Greeks first used the word *adamas*, the root of "diamond," for hard stones that were probably colorless sapphires; later the name was transferred to the even harder diamond. It is doubtful that the ancient Greeks knew diamonds, but Romans certainly did by first to second century A.D.) Ironically the other common natural form of carbon, graphite, is one of the softest known minerals. Graphite forms at lower temperatures and pressures near the Earth's surface, and its carbon atoms are arranged in layers. Weak bonding between layers enables them to easily slide over each other, giving graphite a greasy texture and making it suitable for use in pencil leads and lubricants. Diamond is also the best known conductor of heat, better than any metal, a property that makes it cool to the touch.

Diamond also has a very high refractive index and dispersion, giving rise to the dazzling brilliance and fire of a well-cut stone. As light strikes a gem, some of it is reflected off the surface; the part that enters the stone slows down and is bent from its original path, a phenomenon called refraction. (The apparent bending of a stick in water is caused by refraction, as light slows and changes direction when it enters the water.) The degree to which this happens is known as the refractive index, which is extremely high in diamond relative to most gems. A well-cut diamond takes advantage of this refracting ability and, combined with reflection off the insides of the back facets, directs most of the light entering the stone back out the top, thereby maximizing its brilliance.

Each of the spectral colors that make up white light travels at slightly different speeds and therefore refracts by different amounts when entering a gem; red light, for example, travels faster and consequently bends less than violet light. Thus as light travels through a gem the colors become more and more separated, or dispersed. This spread of light into individual colors that change and flash with every tilt of the stone is called dispersion and, in a gem, is commonly

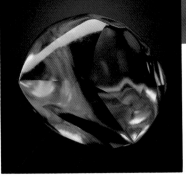

Top:
The extraordinary Oppenheimer Diamond weighs 253.7 carats (3.8 cm or 1.5 in height) and shows the typical octahedral (eight-sided double pyramid) shape of many diamond crystals. It is extremely unusual that a diamond crystal of this size was not cut into gems. The diamond was found at the Dutoitspan mine near Kimberley, South Africa, in 1964. Gift of Harry Winston in honor of Sir Ernest Oppenheimer, former chairman of the board of directors of De Beers Consolidated Mines, Ltd., 1964

Above:
Diamonds were commercially mined near Murfreesboro, Arkansas, in the early 1900s; now visitors to Crater of Diamonds State Park can pay a fee to search for diamonds. This 17.85-carat diamond is one of the largest uncut crystals from this locality

Right:
Light passing through the 16.72-carat Pearson Diamond is dispersed into its spectral colors. In gems, this phenomenon is called fire

referred to as fire. Diamond has a relatively high dispersion, which is enhanced by proper cutting and the fact that the fire shows off well in a colorless gem.

Despite their extreme hardness, diamonds are not indestructible. Hardness is a measure of a material's resistance to scratching. But hit a diamond with a hammer or knock it against a cement wall and it will very likely chip or shatter. Why? There are certain directions through diamond's atomic structure that correspond to layers of atoms that are less strongly linked to each other. When struck by a hard blow, a diamond splits, or cleaves, along these zones of relative weakness. Pliny the Elder in his *Natural History* stated that "These stones are tested upon the anvil, and will resist the blow to such an extent as to make the iron rebound and the very anvil split asunder." Unfortunately, this belief persisted for centuries, and many fine diamonds were reduced to powder as the result of such "testing." Even in the fifteenth century, certain unscrupulous gem merchants convinced Indian miners that stones they had found were not true diamonds by breaking them with a hammer. Of course, after the departure of the disappointed miners, the merchants simply gathered up the larger pieces. Diamond cutters take advantage of diamond's cleavage to split and shape rough diamonds and trim away flawed material. Also, diamonds are not equally hard in all directions, and therefore diamond cutters try to orient gems so that facets correspond to those directions that are easiest to polish.

Measurements from tiny mineral grains that were trapped inside of growing diamond crystals reveal that most diamonds are one to three billion years old (in general, diamonds are probably older than most other important gem minerals, which range in age from millions to billions of years). Once a diamond crystal has formed in the Earth's upper mantle, it might remain there for millions or billions of years before being carried to the surface by molten rock in as little as a few hours, traveling at speeds of up to 70 km (43 mi) per hour. Near the surface, the molten rock erupts explosively and hardens into a type of rock called kimberlite (or, less commonly, lamproite), in which the diamond is embedded. In many places erosion has freed the diamonds from the kimberlite and they accumulate in gravel deposits.

The oldest recorded finds of diamonds date back almost three thousand years to India, and until the early eighteenth century India was the only significant source of diamonds. Famous diamonds such as the Koh-in-noor and Hope Diamond were plucked from the gravels near Golconda, India. After the

The National Gem Collection is noted for its colored diamonds. This spectacular group includes the renowned Blue Heart Diamond (30.82 carats, back row, left); a cognac-colored diamond (36.73 carats, back row, center) cut from a 264-carat crystal and a gift of Mrs. Libbie Moody Thompson, 1991; the delicate yellow Canary Diamond (12.0 carats, back row, right), a gift of Mrs. Oliver B. James; the intense-yellow Shepard Diamond (18.30 carats, middle row, left) from South Africa, which was acquired by exchange for a collection of small diamonds that had been seized as smuggled goods by the United States Customs Service and is named for the Smithsonian employee who helped facilitate the transaction; a lively, intense-pink diamond (2.86 carats, middle row, center) from the Williamson mine in Tanzania and a gift from S. Sydney DeYoung, 1987; the colorless Pearson Diamond (16.72 carats, middle row, right), a gift of Mrs. G. Burton Pearson; and two natural, uncut green diamonds (2.05 and 0.97 carats respectively, front row) from the Modder Deep mine, Cape Province, South Africa and a gift from Dr. G. W. Bain. The green color is caused by trace impurities of uranium

discovery of diamonds in Brazil in 1723, it quickly surpassed India as the most important producer of diamonds. Then, in 1867, diamonds were found in gravels near the Orange River in South Africa. Further explorations in the area uncovered rich deposits that formed the basis of the modern diamond industry. Today Australia (39 percent), Russia (15 percent), Zaire (15 percent), Botswana (14 percent), and South Africa (10 percent) account for about 93 percent of the world's diamond supply. Namibia, Ghana, Brazil, and Gabon account for most of the remaining diamonds, and Canada is rapidly becoming a major source. On the average, 250 tons of kimberlite, or similar rock, must be removed and processed to yield a one-carat gem-quality diamond. It is estimated that throughout history a total of two hundred tons (1.02 billion carats) of diamonds have been mined.

More than three-quarters of all diamonds mined each year go to the Central Selling Organization (De Beers) in London, where diamonds are sorted and sold to diamond cutters around the world. Rough diamonds are accumulated from De Beers's own mines and by buying on the open market. Every five weeks 160 "sightholders" are invited to London to view their allocations. This very controlled distribution system assures relatively stable and uniform diamond prices. Unfortunately this system also makes it nearly impossible to know the origin of any particular diamond, as that information, and production figures in general, are held confidential.

A major factor leading to diamond's popularity as a gem was the development of cutting styles that best display diamond's brilliance and fire. In ancient India, diamonds were not cut because it was believed that this would destroy their magical properties. Simple cutting of diamonds began in Europe around 1300, and commonly only natural crystal faces or broken surfaces were polished. As diamonds became more plentiful, lapidaries experimented with different cuts and learned more about the interplay of light with diamonds. Cardinal Mazarin of France is commonly credited with taking the first step in the middle of the seventeenth century toward the modern brilliant cut with a cushion-shaped cut having thirty-four facets that better showed off diamond's reflectivity, or brightness. Most likely he did not invent the cut, but rather it was named after him because he had one of the most famous diamond collections of the time. (In fact he was one of Jean-Baptiste Tavernier's best customers.) A major advance was introduced by a Venetian lapidary named

Three hundred and twenty-five pear-shaped, baguette, and round brilliant-cut diamonds (totaling 131.4 carats) set in a platinum necklace designed by Harry Winston, Inc. Gift of Mrs. Lita Annenberg Hazen, 1979

The much publicized Victoria-Transvaal Diamond was cut from a 240-carat rough stone found at the Premier mine in Transvaal, South Africa, in 1951. The fancy "champagne-colored" (yellowish brown) stone was originally cut to 75 carats but then recut to better proportions. The nearly flawless pear-shaped gem sports 116 facets and weighs 67.89 carats. The necklace was designed by Baumgold Brothers, Inc., and consists of a yellow-gold chain with sixty-six round brilliant-cut diamonds, fringed with ten drop motifs, each set with two marquise-cut diamonds, a pear-shaped diamond, and a small round brilliant-cut diamond (the total weight of the 106 diamonds is about 45 carats). Gift of Leonard and Victoria Wilkinson, 1977

Peruzzi in 1700 when he cut fifty-eight facets, the same number that is standard for the brilliant cut today. Peruzzi's cut, which had good brilliance but lacked fire, became the standard diamond cut for the next two centuries. A variation is known as the old mine cut. In 1919, Marcel Tolkowsky, a European cutter, worked out the precise angles and proportions for the round brilliant-cut diamond that achieves the best balance of brilliance and fire. Diamonds in modern jewelry most commonly are round brilliant cuts with fifty-eight facets. Popular variations of the brilliant cut include marquise, oval, and

In 1952, thanks to some adroit press-agentry, the Victoria-Transvaal Diamond. starred in RKO's *Tarzan's Savage Fury*, along with Lex Barker and Dorothy Hart

pear shapes. Typically, about 50 percent of the original rough diamond is lost during the cutting of a round brilliant gem. The four major cutting centers today are New York, Antwerp, Tel Aviv, and Bombay.

Finally, the popularity of diamonds is abetted by tradition. The gem became a symbol of love before the Middle Ages, but it was not until 1477, when Archduke Maximilian of Austria gave a diamond ring to Princess Mary of Burgundy, that the tradition of diamond engagement rings began. Aggressive marketing, especially since World War II, has greatly expanded the custom.

Only about 20 percent of mined diamonds are gem quality; the rest are used by industry. Because of their superior hardness, diamonds are used in saws and other cutting tools (such as dentist drills and surgical scapels), as protective coatings on lenses, and as abrasives and polishing compounds. The elec-

Left:

The fifty starburst-cut, fancy-yellow diamonds in a yellow-gold necklace designed by Cartier Inc. in the late 1980s range from about 1.0 to 20 carats and total approximately 245 carats. The matching ear clips each feature 25.3-carat yellow diamonds, and the ring showcases a 61.12-carat yellow diamond. Gift of Mrs. Janet Annenberg Hooker, 1994

A yellow-gold brooch displays a dazzling array of seventy-one fancy-colored diamonds ranging in hue from orange to brown (above). Exposure to ultraviolet light reveals an impressive number of fluorescent gems (left). The marquise-cut, pear-shaped, and round brilliant-cut diamonds range from 0.3 to 2.5 carats and total 61.3 carats. Gift of Leonard and Victoria Wilkinson, 1977

51

The origin of the remarkable Blue Heart Diamond (below) is not known, but it was probably found in South Africa. Atanik Eknayan of Paris cut the 30.82-carat heart-shaped brilliant in 1909–10, and it was purchased by the French jeweler Pierre Cartier in 1910. The following year Cartier sold the gem, set in a lily-of-the-valley brooch, to a Mrs. Unzue of Argentina. The diamond was acquired by Van Cleef & Arpels in 1953 and sold in a pendant to a German baron. In 1959, the Blue Heart Diamond was purchased by Harry Winston, who mounted it in its present ring setting, surrounded by thirty-five white diamonds. Gift of Mrs. Marjorie Merriweather Post, 1964

The cause of the extremely rare deep red color of certain diamonds is not understood, but might be related to defects in the crystals' atomic structure. The gem above is one of the largest known deep red diamonds (5.03 carats). S. Sydney DeYoung, a Boston jeweler, apparently acquired the diamond as part of a collection of estate jewelry, in which it was identified as a garnet hatpin. Gift of S. Sydney DeYoung, 1987

This lively 2.86-carat pink diamond comes from the Williamson mine in Tanzania. Gift of S. Sydney DeYoung, 1963

tronics industry takes advantage of diamond's excellent heat conductivity for use as heat sinks in electronic components. The first synthetic diamonds were made in 1954 by General Electric, and today approximately three-quarters of all industrial diamonds are manufactured. Although gem-quality synthetic diamonds can be produced, they currently are not a threat to the natural diamond market.

Diamonds, of course, are not necessarily colorless; in fact, very few specimens are completely without color. In most diamonds, a few atoms of nitrogen substituted for some of the carbon as the crystals formed, and they interact with light to tint the stones yellow or brown. In general, the more yellow a diamond, the less it is worth, unless the hue is sufficiently intense for the stone to be graded a fancy color, such as the deep yellow 18.30-carat Shepard Diamond in the National Gem Collection. The popularity of colored diamonds has increased dramatically in recent years, and some of the most valuable gemstones are fancy-colored diamonds, especially in shades of blue, pink, and red. In 1987, for example, a red diamond sold at auction for almost a million dollars per carat, and recently a 13.44-carat deep blue diamond sold for $550,000 per carat. By comparison, a flawless, colorless diamond might sell for $25,000 to $50,000 per carat, depending on size and cut.

The National Gem Collection includes the world's finest public display of important colored diamonds. Most famous, of course, is the 45.52-carat steel-blue Hope Diamond. But also on display is one of the world's other great blue diamonds, the Blue Heart. At 30.82 carats, it is two-thirds the size of its bigger blue cousin, but its modern heart-shaped brilliant cut and lively blue color have made it one of the collection's most popular gems. Undoubtedly the rarest diamond in the National Gem Collection is a 5.03-carat deep orange-red gem. It is apparently the largest natural deep red diamond on public display in the world. Red and pink diamonds probably owe their colors to light interacting with defects or mistakes, such as missing atoms, in their crystalline structure. In the past few years, the great Argyle mine in western Australia has become a major source of small (typically less than a few carats) pink to pinkish brown diamonds.

CORUNDUM: RUBY AND SAPPHIRE

Ruby and sapphire are gem varieties of the mineral corundum. Corundum is aluminum oxide and is the second hardest material known, after diamond. Although relatively common, most corundum is not gem quality, and because of its extreme hardness large quantities of it are mined each year for use as polishing compounds and abrasives. Corundum is commonly found where clay-rich limestone was altered into marble by heat and pressure; the aluminum from the clay crystallized as corundum. Corundum is also found in some aluminum-rich igneous rocks. In many of the important gem corundum-producing areas of the world, the durable corundum crystals were released from the host rock by weathering and concentrated in gravel deposits from which the gems are recovered.

Pure corundum is colorless, but even tiny amounts of impurity atoms locked into crystals as they grew can impart a range of vivid colors. For example, just a few atoms per thousand of chromium replacing aluminum are enough to tint corundum the deep red color of ruby, the most prized corundum gem. Iron and titanium, on the other hand, are responsible for the deep blue color of sapphire. Other kinds of impurity atoms can color corundum crystals a range of hues, from pink, yellow, and orange to purple, green, and even black. Corundum gems other than deep red or blue are called fancy sapphires. Corundum gems are commonly pleochroic, that is, they appear different colors when viewed through different directions. For example, rubies typically appear purplish red in one direction and orange-red in the other, and blue sapphires show a greenish blue to violet-blue pleochroism.

The name ruby is from the Latin *ruber*, meaning "red." Historically this gemstone has been called many names, some of which clearly indicate its status as a gem valued over all others. For example, in Sanskrit ruby is known as *ratnaraj*, king of precious stones, or as *ratnanâyaka*, leader of precious stones. According to Hindu lore, the brilliant color of ruby is caused by an inner fire that cannot be extinguished or hidden by clothing or other wrapping. Early Hindu and Burmese miners believed that colorless or pale pink sapphires were rubies that had not fully matured or ripened. To them, the ruby was the most complete and perfect corundum gem. A fine ruby was valued by the Burmese not only for its beauty but also as a talisman of good fortune and bestower of invincibility.

Left:
A 175.1-carat natural sapphire from Sri Lanka shows the typical shape of sapphire crystals. In order to obtain the deepest color, gems are oriented so that the top of the cut stone is perpendicular to the length of the crystal

Below:
Natural ruby crystals on calcite from a mine in Mogok, Burma

Rubies are still one of the most popular and valuable gemstones. The price per carat of a top-quality ruby is rivaled, perhaps, only by that of certain rare, fancy-colored diamonds. A 16-carat Burmese ruby recently sold at auction for more than $225,000 per carat! The most important source of fine rubies since the late fifteenth century has been the region around Mogok, Burma. In fact, the descriptor "Burmese" has become synonymous with the best and most valuable rubies. Burmese rubies are generally considered to be the finest color—red to slightly purplish red and medium-dark in tone, with the vibrancy of the color enhanced by a red fluorescence. This color is called pigeon's blood. Large Burmese rubies are rare; fine quality gems weighing more than a few carats are seldom found, and stones larger than 10 carats are exceptional. A major source of rubies today is Thailand, near the Cambodian border. The stones are typically brownish red and darker than those from Burma and are commonly heat-treated to produce a purer red color. Rubies also are mined in Sri Lanka (they are generally lighter in color than Burmese stones), India, Kenya, Pakistan, Vietnam, and Afghanistan.

Below:
Thirty-one antique-cut Burmese rubies (totaling 60 carats) possessing the deep, highly valued color called pigeon's blood were set into this platinum bracelet by Harry Winston, Inc., in 1950. The accompanying 107 diamonds total 27 carats. Anonymous gift, 1961

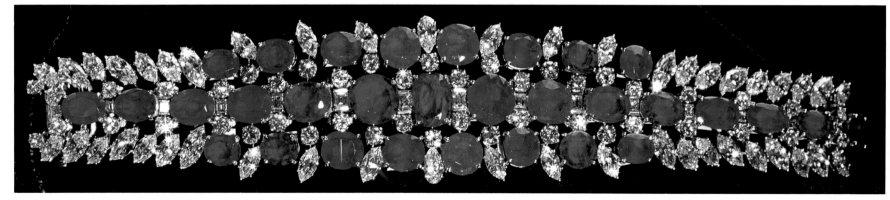

Not until the eighteenth century was it clearly established that sapphires and rubies were close relatives and in fact the same mineral, corundum. Although sapphires occur in a wide variety of colors, traditionally blue has been the most popular and valuable. The noble blue gem, reminiscent of the rich hue of the pure sky, was widely used in jewelry of royalty and was considered the stone most appropriate for ecclesiastical rings. In Europe, during the Middle Ages, sapphires were believed to be an antidote against poisons and endowed with a power to influence the spirits.

Historically the finest sapphire gems came from Sri Lanka and Burma, and the same is pretty much true today. Sri Lanka, nicknamed the "Gem Island," has been an important source of sapphires, rubies, and other gemstones for more than two thousand years. The stones that have eroded from Sri Lanka's central mountains are still plucked by hand from gravel deposits that cover most of the southern half of the island. Sapphires from Sri Lanka are typically light to medium blue, and gemstones have been cut that weigh up to several hundred carats. The National Gem Collection boasts one of the largest fine blue sapphire gems, the 423-carat Logan Sapphire from Sri Lanka.

From 1882 until about 1925 a small region in the Indian state of Kashmir produced sapphires that are velvety, slightly violetish blue in medium to medium-dark tones. Often described as cornflower blue, they are regarded as the finest blue sapphires. Today, Australia and Thailand are the major producers of sapphires. The stones are generally dark to inky blue and anchor the inexpensive to moderate-priced sapphire jewelry market. Recently, China, Kenya, Tanzania, and Nigeria have also become important sources of sapphires. Montana is the only important source of sapphires in the United States.

The majority of fancy-colored sapphires seen in the jewelry trade are from Sri Lanka. Yellow, or golden, and pink are the most common fancy sapphires used in jewelry, but the rarest and most expensive is the pinkish orange variety known as padparadscha, named for a lotus flower whose color it resembles.

Seldom are the ruby and sapphire gems that are sold today the same color as when they came out of the ground. An estimated 90 percent have had their color enhanced, most commonly by heating. Heat treatment of corundum dates back at least two thousand years, and today might be applied by individual miners with charcoal fires and blowpipes or in sophisticated computer-controlled furnaces. The goal of heating is to enrich the color and improve the

Opposite:

An exquisite necklace designed by Harry Winston, Inc., features thirty-six matched sapphires (totaling 195 carats) from Sri Lanka. Their soft, sky blue color is set off by a sea of 435 pear-shaped and round brilliant-cut diamonds (totaling 83.75 carats). Gift of Mrs. Evelyn Annenberg Hall, 1979

Right:

The magnificent 423-carat Logan Sapphire was cut from a crystal mined in Sri Lanka and might be the world's largest faceted blue sapphire (it is about the size of an egg). It is the heaviest mounted gem in the National Gem Collection, and in its brooch setting is framed by twenty round brilliant-cut diamonds, totaling 16 carats. Gift of Mrs. John A. Logan, 1960

Left:
A colorful assortment of sapphires recovered from the gravels of the Missouri River bars near Helena, Montana. They range from about 0.1 to 2.5 carats

Below:
Sapphires ranging from 10.3 to 92.6 carats; the green and large yellow stones are from Burma and the others are from Sri Lanka. Although typically thought of as blue, sapphires exhibit a variety of colors, depending upon the chemical impurities that are present in their atomic structures

Beautiful blue sapphires have been mined from near Yogo Gulch, Montana, since about 1895 and have found their way into the most prestigious gem collections in the world, including the British Crown Jewels. The crystals rarely yield gems larger than a few carats. One of the largest known faceted Yogo sapphires is a 10.2-carat gem (with a large liquid/gas bubble inclusion). The smaller stones range from 1.9 to 2.2 carats

stone's clarity. Many colorless or pale stones can be turned into brilliant blue or yellow sapphires by the application of heat.

Heat treatments of gemstones can produce a variety of results depending upon the starting material and the type of heating process. Sapphires and rubies that appear cloudy due to inclusions of tiny, needlelike crystals of rutile (titanium dioxide, known in the trade as silk) can be improved by heating to 1,000–1,900 °C (1,832–3,452 °F) for several hours and cooling rapidly. The rutile crystals redissolve into the corundum and the stone appears clearer. Pale or colorless sapphires can be transformed to a rich blue color by heating to 1,600–1,900 °C (2,912–3,452 °F) in the absence of oxygen (accomplished by adding charcoal or other carbon-rich material to the heating vessel). This process changes the chemical state of iron impurities in the corundum (from Fe^{+3} to Fe^{+2}). Alternatively, if the heating takes place in an oxidizing atmosphere (with abundant oxygen) the same stones might turn intense yellow (Fe^{+2} is converted to Fe^{+3}). Most yellow sapphire gems have been treated in this way. Rubies are also treated to produce a more attractive red color by heating in an oxidizing atmosphere. This removes any blue tints that might be muddying the color.

The 858-carat uncut Gachala Emerald was found at the Vega de San Juan mine in Gachala, Colombia, in 1967. Rarely are emerald crystals of such size and superb color preserved; usually they are cut into gems. Gift of Harry Winston, 1969

Red beryl crystals, such as this one from Utah, have only been found in the United States. The larger crystal is about 2.5 cm (1 in) long

BERYL: EMERALD, AQUAMARINE, HELIODORE, AND MORGANITE

Emerald is the rich green gem variety of the mineral beryl and one of the most precious gemstones. But beryl is also prized for its other gem varieties: rich blue to blue-green aquamarine, delicate pink morganite, golden yellow heliodore, and rare red beryl. Beryl is beryllium aluminum silicate, and pure crystals are colorless and rare. The rich hues of its gems are caused by a variety of impurity atoms that were incorporated in the crystals as they grew. Emerald's green color is caused by traces of chromium and sometimes vanadium. Aquamarine and heliodore are both tinted by light interacting with traces of iron (Fe^{+2} in aquamarine and Fe^{+3} in heliodore). Morganite and red beryl get their hues from manganese. Although beryl lacks the hardness and fire of some other gems, it more than compensates with its dazzling array of colors.

Emerald is the most valuable beryl gem. As early as 2000 B.C. emeralds were being mined in Egypt. The stones were typically small and of poor quality, but these mines were the major sources of emeralds in the Old World until the sixteenth century. To the Egyptians, the green stones were a symbol of fertility and life. Pliny the Elder described the green color of emeralds as calming and soothing to the eye, a reference that apparently spawned considerable lore in later centuries about the healing powers of the gem, especially for eye ailments.

The finest emeralds are found in the region around Muzo and Chivor, Colombia, where they occur in white calcite or quartz veins in dark shales and limestones. These green gems were used by indigenous peoples for at least one thousand years before the arrival of the Spanish conquistadores in the sixteenth century. Although spurred primarily by their passion for gold and silver, the Spanish quickly recognized the potential of the exquisite green crystals and took control of the mines. Emeralds became popular among European royalty and were shipped from the New World by the boatload. The great richness of the Colombian mines led to a glut of emeralds in Europe, triggering a brisk trade of the gemstones to the Middle East and India. The Mogul rulers in India were especially fond of emeralds and encouraged a vast gem cutting and jewelry industry. Many of the finished pieces were traded back to Europe.

An Art Deco Indian-style necklace (far left) made in 1928–29 by Cartier Inc. features twenty-four baroque-cut emerald drops, each surmounted by a smaller emerald bead, mounted in platinum with pavé-set diamonds. It belonged to Marjorie Merriweather Post, who wore it, dressed as "Juliette," for the Palm Beach Everglades Ball, 1929 (left). The pendant in the photograph was later removed from the necklace and made into a brooch. Gift of Mrs. Marjorie Merriweather Post, 1964

This 21.04-carat Colombian emerald was once set in a ring worn by Mexico's ill-fated Emperor Maximilian, the Austrian archduke who was placed on the throne of Mexico by European intrigue in 1864 and executed during an uprising only three years later. The emerald in its present ring setting by Cartier Inc. is enhanced by six baguette diamonds. Gift of Mrs. Marjorie Merriweather Post, 1964

Above:
The superb clarity and deep green color of the 37.8-carat Chalk Emerald ranks it among the very finest Colombian emeralds. According to legend, it was once was the centerpiece of an emerald and diamond necklace belonging to a maharani of the former state of Baroda in India. It originally weighed 38.4 carats, but was recut and set in a ring, where it is surrounded by sixty pear-shaped diamonds (totaling 15 carats), by Harry Winston, Inc. Gift of Mr. and Mrs. O. Roy Chalk, 1972

Left:
The stunning 168-carat Mackay Emerald was mined in Muzo, Colombia. The largest cut emerald in the National Gem Collection, it is set in an Art Deco diamond and platinum necklace designed by Cartier Inc. In 1931, Clarence H. Mackay presented the necklace as a wedding gift to his wife, Anna Case, a prima donna of the New York Metropolitan Opera from 1909 to 1920. Gift of Mrs. Anna Case Mackay, 1984

Today emerald is one of the most popular, and expensive, gems. Depth of color and clarity are the most important factors that affect value. Unfortunately, treatments to enhance emeralds are rampant: most commonly stones are oiled to mask flaws and deepen color. In addition to Colombia, emeralds are mined in Zambia, Brazil, Russia, Zimbabwe, Pakistan, and Afghanistan. A small number of fine emeralds have been found in North Carolina.

Flawless emeralds, especially stones larger than a few carats, are extremely rare. Many emeralds show cracks and inclusions of fluids and tiny crystals of foreign minerals, collectively referred to in the gem trade somewhat euphemistically as jardins, or gardens. The inclusions can be useful for distinguishing natural from synthetic emeralds. (Synthetic emeralds have the same atomic structure and chemistry as natural gems and have become a booming business.) Also, because certain inclusions are unique to particular emerald deposits, they make it possible to track an emerald gem to its original source. For example the Mackay Emerald in the National Gem Collection contains an inclusion of the mineral parisite, which pinpoints its source as Muzo, Colombia.

The National Gem Collection has a number of outstanding emerald gems. The 38.6-carat Chalk Emerald exhibits the velvety deep green to bluish green color that is most highly prized in Colombian emeralds. The 75.47-carat Hooker Emerald (described in chapter 2) is exceptional for its size and color and for the fact that it is almost devoid of inclusions and other visible flaws. The huge 168-carat Mackay Emerald is the largest cut emerald in the collection.

Aquamarine, as the name suggests, exhibits the variable color of the sea. Its color depends on the relative amounts of impurities of iron in two different chemical states (Fe^{+2} and Fe^{+3}). Heating removes the green tones (by changing Fe^{+3} to Fe^{+2}), leaving a more pure shade of blue. Deep blue is the most highly prized aquamarine color in jewelry. The popularity of aquamarine has been somewhat diminished in the United States in recent years because of the overwhelming availability of similarly colored and less expensive irradiated blue topaz. The state of Minas Gerais in Brazil is by far the leading supplier of gem aquamarine; other significant sources are Pakistan, Nigeria, Russia, and Madagascar, and Maine, Idaho, and California in the United States.

Heliodore, or golden beryl, gets its name from two Greek words meaning sun and gift. The yellow glow comes from iron (Fe^{+3}). Heliodore finds minor use in jewelry, and the most important sources are Brazil and Ukraine. Recently it has

Impurities of iron in different chemical states are responsible for the colors in these aquamarines and green beryls from Brazil, ranging from 911 to 2,054 carats

A pendant/brooch features a superb 216-carat heliodore (golden beryl) from Minas Gerais, Brazil. Gift of Mrs. H. V. Rubin

been the practice to heat Ukrainian heliodore crystals to change them to rich blue aquamarine. Beryl that is colored green to yellow-green by iron, as opposed to the brilliant green induced by chromium in emeralds, is referred to as green beryl.

Morganite, which gets its color from trace quantities of manganese, ranges from pink or rose to peach and was named by the renowned gemologist George Kunz after his patron, financier J. P. Morgan. Madagascar is famous for its deep pink morganite gems, but most stones now come from Brazil or California. Colorless beryl, or goshenite, is rarely cut as gems; it was named for beryl deposits found near Goshen, Massachusetts.

Red beryl, which also is colored by manganese, has only been found in the United States, in Utah and New Mexico. Gems larger than a few carats are rare because the parent crystals are typically small and flawed.

Aquamarine, morganite, and heliodore are found almost exclusively in special kinds of mineral deposits called pegmatites. As large bodies of molten rock solidify beneath the surface of the Earth, the final portion to crystallize is rich in water and rare elements, such as beryllium, lithium, and boron, and has a special chemistry that encourages rapid growth of gigantic mineral crystals. The resulting pegmatite deposits are important sources for many rare minerals and gems. Aquamarine and green beryl crystals weighing up to several hundred kilograms have been found in pegmatites, giving rise to some giant gems, such as the 2,054- and 1,000-carat stones in the National Gem Collection. These oversized gems, although not suitable for use in jewelry, make stunning exhibition pieces.

Morganite gems ranging from 56 to 331.4 carats show the range of hues for this pink variety of beryl; the purple-pink gem in the front-left and deep pink stone at right are from Madagascar, the others are from Brazil

4. Other Important Gems

QUARTZ:
AMETHYST, SMOKY QUARTZ, ROCK CRYSTAL, CITRINE, ROSE QUARTZ, CHALCEDONY, AGATE, AND JASPER

Quartz is one of the most abundant minerals in the Earth's crust. It is the major constituent of beach sand and an important component of many types of rocks. Quartz is composed of the elements silicon and oxygen and in its pure state is colorless, but just small amounts of various impurity atoms can yield a range of vivid colors. The profusion of colors, patterns, and textures displayed by quartz is unmatched by any other mineral, and makes it one of the most widely used gem materials. Quartz derives its name from a Slavic word meaning "hard." The Greeks referred to quartz as *krystallos*, meaning "ice." They assumed quartz crystals were ice that was frozen so solid that it would not melt, a belief that persisted into the Middle Ages. The Greek name for quartz is the origin of the word *crystal*.

Quartz gems fall into two groupings. The first grouping consists of those cut from individual crystals of quartz and includes amethyst, smoky quartz, rock crystal, citrine, and rose quartz. The so-called fine-grained varieties make up the second group and are compact aggregates of tiny fibrous or granular quartz crystals. The separate crystals can only be distinguished with the aid of a microscope. The different varieties of fine-grained quartz, such as chalcedony, agate, flint, and jasper, correspond to particular textures and colors. Recent studies have shown that most so-called fine-grained quartz also contains a varying percentage of the newly described mineral moganite intimately intergrown with the quartz. Moganite is also silicon dioxide, but has a different atomic structure from that of quartz.

Under ideal conditions, in spacious cavities or other openings in rock, quartz crystals can grow impressively large, sometimes weighing several tons. Clear, colorless quartz, called rock crystal, is the most common gem mineral. But because of its low refractive index, it lacks brilliance and fire and has a glassy appearance, and therefore is rarely used as a gemstone. More commonly, rock crystal is used for carvings, chandeliers, and of course, crystal balls. The National Gem Collection has the largest known flawless quartz sphere, 32.8 cm (12.9 in) in diameter and weighing 48.4 kg (106.7 lb).

Page 70 and below:
The world's largest flawless quartz sphere was cut and polished in China in 1923–24; it weighs 48.4 kg (106.7 lb) and measures 32.8 cm (12.9 in) in diameter. The original quartz crystal from which the sphere was cut probably came from Burma. Gift of Mrs. Worcester Reed Warner, 1930

Amethyst is the most prized gem variety of quartz. According to Roman mythology, amethyst was colored purple by the god of wine and was thought to offer protection against drunkenness. It derives its name from a Greek word meaning "not to intoxicate." It is now known that just a few iron atoms replacing some of the silicon in quartz cause the purple color. Natural radiation from surrounding rocks where the quartz crystals grew changed these impurity atoms into a special form of iron (Fe^{+4}) that absorbs all colors of light except blue and red, which are reflected back to our eyes, giving rise to

A 36.2-carat amethyst from Delaware County, Pennsylvania contains a swarm of tiny inclusions of gas and liquid that were trapped in the crystal as it grew

amethyst's purple color. The iron impurities are commonly concentrated in layers, or zones, in amethyst crystals, and therefore many amethyst gemstones, when viewed in certain directions, show alternating colorless and purple bands. Amethyst is commonly heat-treated to improve its color.

Amethyst is found in a variety of geologic settings, but the most important is as crystals lining cavities in volcanic rock, such as in southern Brazil and Uruguay. This region is by far the major source of gem amethyst. About 130 million years ago gas bubbles were trapped in cooling volcanic lava and formed cavities up to several meters in diameter. Later water percolated through the rock, dissolving silica and depositing it as amethyst crystals lining the insides of the cavities. Only flawless amethyst with intense color is cut into gemstones; the remainder is sold to collectors or as decorative pieces.

Citrine is the golden yellow to orange gem variety of quartz. The name comes from the French *citron*, meaning "lemon," in reference to its color. Like

Part amethyst and part citrine, these 24.2 (left) and 55.7-carat ametrine gems are from Bolivia. Gifts of Ray Meisenholder and John W. May, respectively

This assortment of quartz gems exhibits a variety of cutting styles and includes amethyst (purple), rose quartz (pink), citrine (gold-yellow), smoky quartz (gray-black), and rock crystal (colorless). The largest gem—the shield-shaped citrine (center top)—is 636 carats

amethyst, citrine is colored by impurities of iron, but the iron is in a different chemical state (Fe^{+3}). Natural citrine crystals are relatively rare, mostly found in Brazil and Madagascar, and most gem material is amethyst turned yellow by heating. Citrine is popular in jewelry, but is sometimes confused with topaz.

Smoky quartz ranges in color from light gray-brown and smoke yellow to black, and is colored by impurities of aluminum combined with the effects of

natural radiation. The radiation causes defects (it removes an electron from an oxygen atom adjacent to one of the aluminum atoms) in the atomic structure that absorb all colors of light, producing the dark color. Much of the smoky quartz used as gems is produced by artificially irradiating colorless quartz crystals. (Both the natural and irradiated crystals lose their color if heated.) Smoky quartz is a traditional gemstone of Scotland, where it is called cairngorm after sources in the Cairngorm Mountains. Large gems are common, but the color is not currently popular in fashion jewelry. Brazil is the major supplier of smoky quartz; other well-known sources are the Swiss Alps, Russia, and Madagascar.

Above left:
A band of rose quartz crystals grew on a previously formed smoky quartz crystal in this specimen from the Sapucaia mine, Minas Gerais, Brazil; it is affectionately known to some as the "pink tutu"

Above right:
Smoky-citrine quartz crystals from Minas Gerais, Brazil. The nearly flawless crystals weigh 53 kg (117 lb). Gift of the Independent Jewelers Organization

Rose quartz ranges in color from pale pink to deep rose red. It typically is found in massive chunks and rarely occurs as individual crystals. Most rose quartz appears turbid, and deep-colored, flawless material is uncommon. Consequently it is more suited for beads and carvings than faceted gemstones. The cause of the color in rose quartz continues to be somewhat of a puzzle for scientists. Recent studies indicate that some material is probably colored by impurities of aluminum and phosphorous, but in other cases minute crystals of other minerals trapped in the quartz likely play a role. Rose quartz is found almost exclusively in pegmatite deposits, and the most important sources are Brazil and Madagascar.

Mineral crystals trapped within quartz crystals as they grew also contribute to the array of quartz gems. For example, colorless quartz enclosing needles of golden rutile or black tourmaline can be cut into attractive cabochons. Aventurine is a variety of green, sparkly quartz containing tiny platelike crystals of a green mica called fuchsite. Gem aventurine comes primarily from India and is fashioned into beads, cabochons, and carvings.

The popular gemstone known as tiger's eye is formed when a variety of asbestos (blue asbestos) called crocidolite is naturally replaced, atom by atom, by quartz. The resulting material retains crocidolite's original fibrous texture, which gives rise to the intriguing play of light, or chatoyancy, in polished stones. The brown color is caused by minute particles of the mineral goethite (iron oxide hydroxide), a residue from the breakdown of the crocidolite. In cases where not all of the crocidolite has been replaced by quartz, the gemstone has a bluish hue and is called hawk's eye. South Africa produces most tiger's eye and hawk's eye.

The fine-grained varieties of quartz are prized for their seemingly limitless combination of colors and patterns that uncannily mimic, and have in some cases perhaps inspired, a range of artistic styles. Western landscapes, contemporary designs, and scenes resembling works of the great Impressionists all have been executed by nature in the quartz medium. Because these materials tend to be translucent or opaque, they are typically cut as cabochons or beads, or carved. Depending upon the nature of the quartz microcrystals that comprise them, these gems can be divided into two groups: chalcedony and chert.

Chalcedony is the general term used for all varieties of fine-grained quartz that are built up of thin layers of fibrous quartz crystals. It is typically translucent and has a waxy texture. Chalcedony's fibrous texture makes it extremely tough and therefore an excellent carving and bead material. Some varieties of chalcedony that exhibit characteristic colors and patterns have been given special names. Carnelian is red chalcedony, colored by inclusions of hematite (iron oxide); stones showing a more brownish tone are called sard. The beautiful apple-green chalcedony, called chrysoprase, is tinted by minute crystals

A cut and polished agate from Chihuahua, Mexico

This snuff bottle of Australian chrysoprase with a ruby crystal stopper was carved by Mrs. Helen Hanke

of a nickel mineral. Cameos are ornaments commonly carved in relief out of chalcedony with alternating dark and light bands. The sculptor skilfully uses one colored layer as a background for the other, in which the design has been carved. The red and white variety is called sardonyx.

Agate, with its often dramatic concentric color bands, is probably the most familiar type of chalcedony. Its toughness and beauty make it a popular gemstone among amateur lapidaries. Agates are typically white, gray, and yellowish brown to reddish brown, but shades of blue and green are sometimes also observed. The colors are mostly caused by tiny crystals of iron and manganese oxide minerals in the chalcedony. Agates are commonly found in cavities in volcanic rock, where silica-rich water deposited quartz crystals layer by layer parallel to the cavity wall. The myriad colors and patterns have given rise to many agate names, many used only locally, such as eye agate, crazy lace agate, Laguna agate, and so forth. Moss agate is technically not agate, but white to clear chalcedony containing dendritic, or treelike, growths of black manganese oxide or reddish iron oxide minerals.

Although agates occur worldwide, Brazil is the major commercial source. Much of the material is shipped to Idar-Oberstein, Germany, itself a famous source of agate, for cutting and carving. Because chalcedony is porous and therefore readily stained or dyed, very little finished agate retains its natural color.

The chert varieties of fine-grained quartz consist of nearly equidimensional quartz microcrystals, imparting a granular or sugary texture. Chert is virtually opaque, with a dull luster, and, although commonly white to gray or brown, is found in a range of colors. Flint is a dark gray to black variety of chert typically found in chalk deposits. Jasper is red to reddish brown chert and the most important variety used for ornamental purposes. The many colors and patterns shown by jasper have inspired a plethora of descriptive names, such as picture, leopard-skin, or Bruneau Canyon jasper. Jasper is popular for use in carvings, inlays, and mosaics. Bloodstone is a dark green jasper with blood red flecks that is found primarily in India.

In addition to its use as a gem material, quartz also is an important raw material for the glass and electronic industries, among others. When an electric potential is applied to a quartz wafer of the appropriate thickness, it vibrates at a particular frequency. This piezoelectric property is the basis for the use of quartz crystals in clocks and for controlling frequencies in radios. Since World War II, most quartz used in watches and radios has been synthetic. Synthetic quartz, which has the same atomic structure as natural quartz, is rarely used for gems because the natural stones are so plentiful.

A microscope reveals the fibrous quartz crystals, perpendicular to the banding, that make up the layers in an agate from California. (The field of view is 2.0 mm)

The iridescent colors in fire agate (right) are caused by light scattering off a thin layer of goethite in the chalcedony. This specimen is from Arizona. Light scattering off closely spaced layers of quartz crystals in iris agate (below) also produces iridescent colors. This specimen is from Montana

A 7,500-carat faceted quartz egg from California is an outstanding example of the gem cutter's art. Faceted by John Sinkankas

Until the 1950s, topaz was known almost exclusively as a yellow to golden gemstone. But since then, the routine radiation and heat treatment of pale-colored topaz to turn it deep blue has changed, perhaps forever, the public's perception of this gem. To most of the present generation of jewelry buyers, topaz is recognized primarily as an affordable blue gemstone.

In ancient times all yellow stones were known as topaz, a name probably derived from Topazios, the early Greek name for the island of Zabargad in the Red Sea. The island is famous as a source of peridot, suggesting that the name topaz was once also used for that gemstone. Alternatively, the name might derive from the Sanskrit *tapaz*, meaning "fire." In any case, the name was not exclusively linked to the mineral we know today as topaz until the mid-eighteenth century.

The highly prized imperial topaz is intense golden to reddish orange and is found primarily at Ouro Preto, Brazil. More commonly topaz is colorless to pale blue or yellow. Pink or red stones are rare, although pink stones can be produced by heating the golden brown topaz from Ouro Preto. Some topaz, such as the sherry-colored crystals from Japan and Ukraine, tends to fade permanently to near colorlessness upon exposure to light, especially sunlight. Topaz is one of the hardest gemstones (only diamond, corundum, and chrysoberyl are harder), but its tendency to split or cleave makes it somewhat fragile. The most important sources of gem topaz are Brazil, Russia, Ukraine, and Pakistan.

Topaz is constructed of atoms of aluminum, silicon, fluorine, and oxygen. It typically forms from fluorine-rich solutions and is most abundantly found in pegmatite deposits. Topaz is renowned for its ability to grow huge gem-quality crystals. The current world record holder is a 271 kg (597 lb) giant from a pegmatite deposit in Brazil, and several crystals over 50 kg (110 lb), also from Brazil, are known, including two in the National Gem and Mineral Collection that weigh in at 69.5 kg and 50.4 kg (153 lb and 111 lb), respectively. Not surprisingly, topaz also holds the record for the world's largest faceted gemstone, a whopping 36,854 carats (7.37 kg or 16.2 lb). The largest gem in the National Gem Collection is a pale yellow topaz that weighs 22,892.5 carats (4.6 kg or 10.1 lb).

Two of the finest large topaz crystals known weigh 31.8 kg (70 lb) and 50.4 kg (111 lb) respectively and were mined in Minas Gerais, Brazil. Before being donated to the Smithsonian Institution they had been slated to be cut up for use in scientific instruments. Fortunately, the crystals were spared by the discovery of a more suitable material. At 22,892.5 carats (4.6 kg or 10.1 lb), the American Golden Topaz is one of the world's largest gems. It was cut in the late 1980s by Leon Agee from an 11.8 kg (26 lb) stream-rounded cobble also found in Minas Gerais. The gem sports 172 facets and measures 17.53 x 14.94 x 9.34 cm (6.9 x 5.9 x 3.7 in). Crystals: gifts of Joseph M. Linsey, 1981 (left), and Howard G. Freeman, 1981, (right); gem: gift of the rockhound hobbyists of America through the efforts of the six regional federations of mineralogical societies and Drs. Marie and Ed Borgatta, 1988

Topaz gems in various colors from Russia, Texas, Japan, Madagascar, and Brazil, ranging in size from 18 to 816 carats

Left:
A football-shaped blue topaz gem from Minas Gerais, Brazil, weighs 7,033 carats; like most blue topaz, its color is the result of irradiation and heat treatment. Originally this topaz was probably colorless or very pale yellow-brown

Below:
A pale golden topaz sphere weighing 12,555 carats has more than a thousand facets and was cut in the famous gem-cutting city of Idar-Oberstein, Germany. It was fashioned from a crystal fragment in the National Gem and Mineral Collection

The highly prized imperial topaz is found at Ouro Preto, Brazil. This crystal and gem weigh 875.4 and 93.6 carats respectively

Probably the reason that several large gem-quality topaz crystals can be found in museums is that at the time they were discovered, their pale color made them unattractive for cutting into gems. Such would not be the case today. Large, gemmy, pale crystals are the essential raw material for the modern blue topaz market. Exposure to high-energy radiation, either in a nuclear reactor or linear accelerator, creates defects in topaz's atomic structure and turns the crystals brown. Next, heating the topaz heals the portion of defects that cause the brown color, leaving only those that interact with light to give a blue tint. The blue color is stable and ranges in intensity depending upon the composition of the original topaz and the treatment procedure.

Some natural blue topaz is found in Brazil and Russia, and a number of other places, but the crystals and resulting gemstones are typically very lightly colored. It is believed that natural radiation from rocks surrounding the growing topaz crystals caused the color. It is a safe bet that any deep blue topaz gemstones have been artificially treated.

GARNET

Garnets are familiar to most people as dark red gemstones that were fashionable in the eighteenth and nineteenth centuries and are popular today in moderately priced jewelry. But, in fact, the name garnet refers to an entire family of fifteen distinct minerals, five of which are commonly used as gemstones, and they can exhibit the complete spectrum of colors except blue. All members of the garnet family are closely related in that they are constructed of the same basic arrangement of atoms, but they differ in chemical composition. The color of a garnet is determined by its composition. Garnet minerals are typically found in rocks that have been altered by heat and pressure within the earth or in pegmatite deposits.

The name garnet comes from the Latin *granatum,* meaning "seedlike," because small garnet crystals were thought to resemble reddish-colored pomegranate seeds. Historically garnets have been called carbuncles, from the Latin for "little spark," a term once applied to all bright red gems; today it is used only for dark red garnets cut in the cabochon form with the backs hollowed out to thin them and lighten the color. The use of garnets as gems goes back thousands of years to the early Egyptians, and they were prized by the Greeks and Romans.

Most of the red "garnet" gems used in jewelry are the minerals almandine and pyrope. Pure almandine is iron aluminum silicate and pyrope is magnesium aluminum silicate. Natural almandine garnets, however, always contain some magnesium, and pyrope garnets always have some iron. Iron is primarily responsible for almandine's red color, and iron along with chromium give pyrope its rich hue. Almandine is the most common garnet used in jewelry today, and for most people its name is synonymous with garnet. Almandine is dark red to brownish or purplish red, and because it is abundant, gemstones are generally inexpensive. The most important sources of gem almandine are India, Sri Lanka, and Brazil. Almandine is sufficiently hard and tough that nongem-quality material is mined for use as abrasives, for example, garnet sandpaper.

Pyrope garnets are most commonly seen in antique jewelry, especially from the Victorian period. Limited availability precludes widespread use in modern jewelry. Pyrope gems are typically very dark red to slightly brownish red and

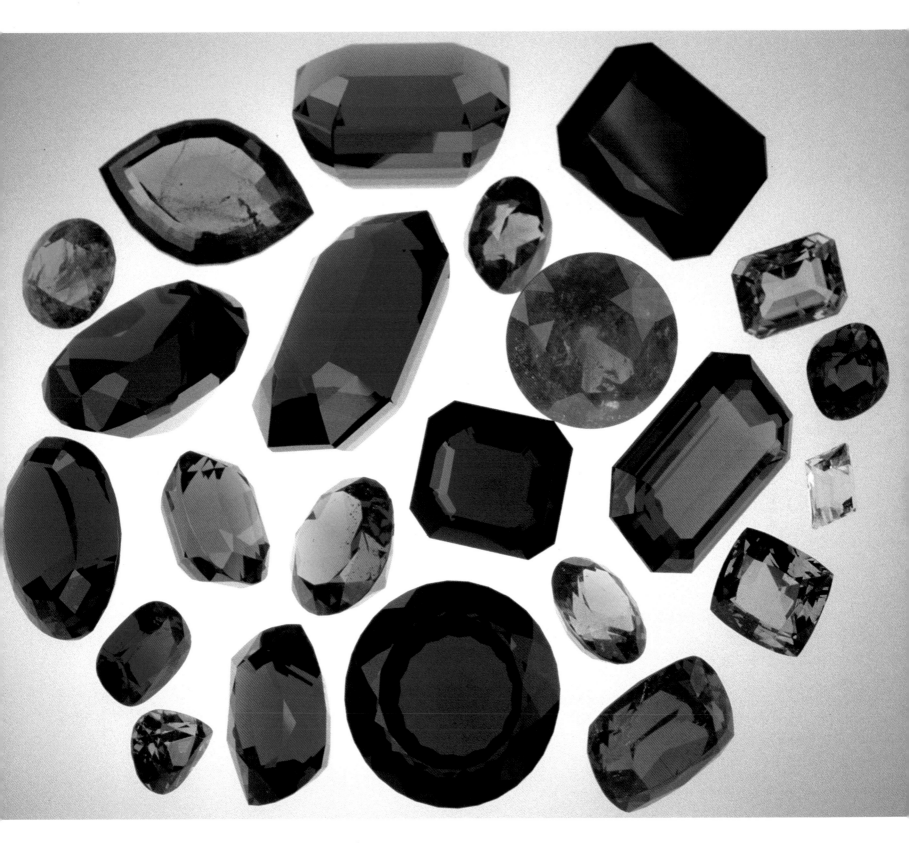

These grossular garnets, averaging about one-half carat, are all from one area in Tanzania/Kenya. Gift of Hans-Dieter Haag

This beautiful 30-carat grossular garnet was found near Ratnapura, Sri Lanka, in 1991 in a small mine on a rubber plantation. Gift of Barry J. Whittle, 1996

seldom are larger than a few carats. Until the late nineteenth century, Bohemia (in what is now the Czech Republic) was the main source of pyrope gems. The most important sources today are the diamond kimberlites of South Africa and Russia; in the United States gem pyropes have been produced from Arizona, New Mexico, and Utah. Pyrope derives its name from the Greek *pyropos,* meaning "firelike."

Around the end of the nineteenth century, attractive raspberry pink to purplish red garnets were found in North Carolina that had compositions intermediate between almandine and pyrope. They were called rhodolite garnets because their color resembled that of the blossoms of the local rhododendron plant. They are a variety of either almandine or pyrope, depending on the proportion of iron to magnesium, which can vary from stone to stone even within a single locality. Today, rhodolite garnets are plentiful and affordable and have become popular in fashion jewelry. The most important sources are Tanzania, India, and Sri Lanka.

Grossular is the garnet mineral that shows the widest range of colors. As pure calcium aluminum silicate it is colorless, but a host of different impurities can tint it shades of pink, orange, reddish orange, yellow, brown, or even green. The name is taken from the botanical name for gooseberry, *Ribes grossularia,* because the first grossular garnets described were a pale green similar to that of the plant's fruit. Reddish to yellowish orange grossular garnets, mostly from Sri Lanka and Brazil, are popularly called hessonite or cinnamon stone, and are sometimes used in jewelry.

The most prized grossular gem in jewelry today, however, is the brilliant green variety called tsavorite, first discovered in 1968 in Kenya's Tsavo National Park. This region on the Kenya-Tanzania border remains the only source of gem tsavorite. The most desirable tsavorite gemstones are such intense green to yellow-green that they can be confused with emerald. The green color is caused by small amounts of vanadium that were incorporated in the garnet crystal as it grew.

The rarest and most valuable garnet gem is the green to greenish yellow variety of the mineral andradite (calcium iron silicate), called demantoid. The name comes from the Old German *Demant,* meaning "diamond," so called because of demantoid's high luster and dispersion. In fact, demantoid's dispersion, or ability to separate light into its component colors, is greater than that of diamond. It was first discovered in Russia's Ural Mountains in 1851.

The fourteen pear-shaped tsavorite garnets in this necklace total 30.8 carats. Gift of Dr. Bray O. Hawk, 1981

Above right:
The pyrope garnets in an antique hairpin are from the Czech Republic, historically the principal source of garnets that were popular in Victorian jewelry

George Kunz, the chief gem buyer for Tiffany & Company in the late nineteenth century, was fascinated by the gem and bought all the demantoid rough he could find. Consequently, Tiffany's made extensive use of demantoid gems in its jewelry during the period. Demantoid gemstones larger than a few carats are rare.

Today, because of limited supplies, demantoid maintains its status as a rare and expensive gem and is most commonly seen in antique jewelry. The major source is still the Ural Mountains, with minor production from Italy and Korea. Demantoid owes its green color to impurities of chromium. Depending upon its chemical composition, andradite garnets also can be brown, yellow, or black, although in these colors it is not normally used for gemstones.

Spessartine is the manganese-rich member of the garnet family and typically is colored yellowish to reddish orange. Spessartine gems can be quite attractive, but they are not commonly used in jewelry because supplies are limited, mostly coming from Sri Lanka, Brazil, and the United States. In the early 1970s pinkish to reddish or yellowish orange garnets were discovered in Tanzania that are intermediate in composition between spessartine and pyrope. They have found some popularity in the gem markets under the name Malaia garnets. (*Malaia* is Swahili for "outcast;" these garnets were initially rejected by the gem markets.)

TOURMALINE

The tourmaline family consists of ten distinct minerals, but only one, elbaite, accounts for nearly all of the tourmaline gemstones. Tourmaline gems cover the complete range of the color spectrum, but in exquisite shades unlike those of any other gem material. Moreover, single crystals of elbaite can show several colors, either along their lengths or from the inside out, making it possible to cut unique multicolored gems.

It seems astonishing that history makes no references to tourmaline as a mineral group or gem before the eighteenth century. It was first identified from a parcel of stones sent to Holland from Sri lanka in 1703. The parcel was simply labeled *turmali,* a Sinhalese term for mixed precious stones. As the story goes, Dutch children playing with the stones noticed that as some of the crystals became heated by the sun they attracted particles of dirt and dust. This strange behavior prompted an investigation that led to the recognition of the new mineral group, called tourmaline after the original label on the parcel. The unusual attractive powers first noticed by the Dutch children is caused by a phenomenon called pyroelectricity. As a consequence of its atomic structure, a tourmaline crystal develops positive and negative electric charges on either end when heated. The crystal attracts the dust for the same reason that dust clings to statically charged clothing. Tourmaline crystals also possess the special ability to acquire an electric charge when struck by an object or subjected to high pressure, such as the shock wave from an explosion: this is called piezoelectricity.

In 1890, John Ruskin's response to a query about tourmaline's chemical composition was: "A little of everything . . . the chemistry is more like a medieval doctor's prescription than the making of a respectable mineral." All tourmaline minerals have the same basic atomic arrangement, and they all contain boron, oxygen, and silicon, combined with other elements. Variations in composition give rise to the different minerals and the impressive range of colors. The atomic structure of tourmalines also accommodates a wide variety of impurity atoms, which greatly increases the color palette. Multicolored crystals formed when the source solution, and consequently the crystals, changed composition as they grew.

Although best known in shades of green and red, elbaite also can be blue, purple, yellow, or colorless. Colored varieties of elbaite are sometimes referred

Far left:
Bicolored elbaite crystal and gem (34.6 carats) from Brazil. Tourmaline crystals are commonly multicolored, reflecting slight changes in composition that occurred as they grew

Left:
An elegant carving in elbaite from Mozambique stands 5.3 cm (2.1 in) high

Below:
A slice cut from a liddicoatite crystal from Madagascar reveals complex changes in the crystal's composition and color that occurred as it grew

to by names, such as rubellite (red-pink), indicolite (blue), and achroite (colorless). Most tourmaline gemstones are strongly pleochroic—the hue and/or intensity of color appears different as the stones are viewed in different directions. Consequently, gem cutters must take care to orient the stones to show the most desirable color. Virtually all gem elbaite is mined from pegmatites, special mineral deposits that are characterized by large mineral crystals and are rich in unusual elements such as boron and lithium—both essential ingredients in elbaite. Today Brazil is by far the greatest producer of gem elbaite; other important sources include the United States (Maine and California), Sri Lanka, Madagascar, Mozambique, Afghanistan, Tanzania, and Russia. Elbaite is named for the source from which it was first described, Italy's island of Elba.

Liddicoatite is the only other tourmaline mineral that finds significant use in the gem trade. It has a chemical composition similar to that of elbaite (elbaite is sodium-rich and liddicoatite is calcium-rich) and shows a comparable assortment of hues. Liddicoatite is named for the American gemologist Richard Liddicoat, and most gem-quality material comes from pegmatite deposits in Madagascar.

Tourmaline crystals were classified as strategic materials during World War II because their piezoelectric behavior made them ideally suited for making pressure gauges to measure the intensities of explosions during weapons' testing, including the first atomic bomb. The piezoelectric property of tourmaline is also the source of the spark provided by igniters for gas barbeque grills and stoves; a charge builds up when pressure is applied to a small piece of a tourmaline crystal.

The many hues of elbaite are shown in a selection of gems ranging from 6.7 to 109 carats from Brazil, Madagascar, the United States, and Afghanistan. The neon-blue stone (below center) is from Paraiba, Brazil, and owes its color to copper

PERIDOT

More than three thousand years ago Egyptians fashioned beads from golden green crystals mined from fissures and cavities on a small, desolate island in the Red Sea. Known to the Greeks and Romans as Topazios, this island has been one of the most important sources for fine peridot, the gem variety of the mineral forsterite (magnesium silicate), a member of the olivine mineral family. Originally called topazion, after the island, this gem eventually was known simply as topaz. In the eighteenth century, for some unexplained reason, that name was transferred to a different gem, our topaz of today, and the name peridot was adopted. The Red Sea island also has been known by several names: St. John's Island, Zebirget, and today as Zabargad, the Arabic name for peridot. Zabargad is still an important source of peridot, along with Burma, the United States (Arizona), Norway, Brazil, Australia, and recently Pakistan.

Pure forsterite is colorless, but iron atoms replacing some of the magnesium produce the green shades; the more iron, the darker the color. Typically in peridot gemstones, iron replaces about 10 percent of the magnesium. Too much iron results in unattractive dark-colored stones with brown tones. Forsterite is common in volcanic basalts and is the major component of special igneous rocks called peridotites, but crystals suitable for cutting into gemstones are rare. Forsterite is also a major component of the Earth's upper mantle, pieces of which are sometimes brought to the surface by volcanic eruptions (such is the case for peridot from Arizona).

Peridot is most prized when dark green without undertones of yellow or brown. It is a relatively soft gemstone, and therefore cut stones tend to lose their polish and become scratched with time. Peridot has a distinctly oily appearance, and the relatively high birefringence (that is, the property of light when traveling through certain directions in the crystal to split into two paths, producing two separate images) causes the edges of the back facets to appear doubled when viewed through the thickness of the stone.

From early times peridot has been associated with the sun and was believed to have medicinal powers. During the Crusades, an abundance of peridot was brought back to Europe, and it was commonly used to adorn religious objects. It was also highly prized by the sultans of the Ottoman Empire. Peridot became popular in jewelry in Europe and the United States in the late nineteenth century.

Opposite left:
The gem-quality forsterite (peridot) nodules in this specimen of basalt from Arizona are fragments of the Earth's upper mantle carried to the surface by volcanic eruption

Opposite right:
Five continents are represented in this impressive array of peridot gems. The gem (34.65 carats) in the necklace is from Arizona. Clockwise from upper right: a 311.8-carat stone from Zabargad, Egypt, which is one of the largest peridot gems known; a gem (103.2 carats) from either Burma or Egypt; a gem (18.13 carats) from a relatively new source in Pakistan; a rare gem (3.02 carats) from McMurdo Sound, Antarctica; a gem (4.08 carats) from Norway; another gem (8.93 carats) from Arizona; another gem (122.7 carats) from either Burma or Egypt; and a 286.6-carat gem from Burma

ZIRCON

Zircon can be found as tiny crystals in most beach sands and granites, but large, gem-quality crystals are scarce. Most gem zircons are found as waterworn pebbles in gravel deposits in Thailand, Cambodia, Vietnam, and Sri Lanka and are typically brown, reddish brown, green, or yellow. Since the 1920s virtually all zircon gemstones used in jewelry have been heat-treated to enhance their colors. Heating in an oxygen-free atmosphere, commonly using simple coal-burning ovens, produces blue zircons, which can then be heated in air to give a golden color. The treatment process also yields some colorless stones.

Zircon is ideally zirconium silicate, but natural crystals almost always contain minor amounts of the element halfnium, which, along with uranium and thorium, is responsible for the color diversity. Radioactivity emitted by the latter two elements can create defects in the atomic structure of zircon and eventually destroy it. The resulting metamict, or noncrystalline, zircons typically are cloudy and pale green and are more brittle than unaltered stones. Often, heating can restore the original crystalline structure and color.

Colorless zircon outperforms any other mineral at imitating diamond. Zircon's dispersion and brilliance is almost as good as that of diamond. Its inferior hardness and brittleness, however, reveal zircon as an imposter. The facet edges on zircon gems are prone to chipping, and polished faces will dull with wear. Nonetheless, well-cut zircons are beautiful gems in their own right. It is unfortunate that zircon's reputation as a diamond simulant has undermined its popularity. Zircons are typically cut as round brilliants, for the same reason as diamond—to best show their brilliance and dispersion, or fire. In the United States the most popular zircons are the blue, colorless, and golden gems produced by heating.

In addition to its use as a gem, zircon is also the major source of the metal zirconium, which because of its corrosion resistance and strength at high temperatures is used to clad the interiors of nuclear reactors. Cubic zirconia is a form of zirconium oxide having a cubic crystal structure; it usually has minor amounts of calcium, magnesium, or yttrium added to stabilize it. It was originally synthesized for use as a high-temperature ceramic, and it wasn't until 1969 that crystals large enough to cut as gems were grown. Cubic zirconia's brilliance and fire are similar to that of diamond, but it is not as hard and is considerably more dense.

Opposite top:
Zircons (left to right) from Thailand (103.2 and 106.1 carats) and Sri Lanka (48.2 and 97.6 carats). Heat treatment of natural reddish brown stones yielded these brilliant gems

Opposite bottom:
A Burmese gold bracelet with natural spinel crystals. The high luster and perfect octahedral crystals of spinel found in the Mogok region of Burma are called by the Burmese "Anyon nat thwe"—spinels that have been cut and polished by the spirits

SPINEL

Many of the world's most famous "rubies" are in fact red spinels. The magnificent 170-carat Black Prince Ruby that dominates the British Imperial Crown is a spinel, as is the Timur Ruby, bearing six Persian inscriptions, in the private collection of Queen Elizabeth II. Both of these stones probably originated from Balascia (now Badakhshan), Afghanistan, the major source of so-called Balas rubies (spinels) during medieval times. They were mined prior to the fourteenth century. It was not until 1783 that spinel was recognized as a mineral distinct from corundum (ruby and sapphire).

As one might suspect from the historical confusion between spinel and ruby, these two gemstones have many similarities. Ruby is aluminum oxide and spinel is magnesium aluminum oxide, and both owe their red color to trace impurities of chromium. They both form when impure limestone is altered by heat and pressure, and they commonly are found side by side. Both minerals are hard and yield durable gems, although corundum is slightly harder. Like corundum, pure spinel is colorless, but chemical impu-

rities give rise to a range of colored gemstones, most typically pink or red, purple, green, and blue.

Red spinels are the most popular in jewelry, but in general the gem-buying public is unfamiliar with spinels. Undoubtedly the historical confusion with ruby has led to its reputation as that gemstone's poor relation. Its many attractive colors and durability make spinel a gem that deserves to be appreciated in its own right. The major sources of spinel gemstones are the gem gravels of Sri Lanka, Burma, and Thailand; other significant occurrences are in Pakistan, Afghanistan, and Russia. Synthetic spinels are sometimes used as a simulant for other gems, such as aquamarine and blue zircon.

Some of the most popular colors of spinel are illustrated by a rosy pink 22.2-carat gem, a ruby red 36.1-carat gem, and a purple-blue 22.1-carat gem. The stone in the center is from Burma, the others are from Sri Lanka

Chrysoberyl is noted for its three beautiful gem varieties. Most commonly it is found as greenish yellow crystals that can yield hard, brilliant faceted gems. These stones were popular in eighteenth- and nineteenth-century Spanish and Portuguese jewelry and in Victorian England, but today are not widely used. The most extraordinary, and valuable, chrysoberyl gems are alexandrite and cat's eyes.

Chrysoberyl is beryllium aluminum oxide and is colorless when pure. Trace amounts of iron color the mineral shades of yellow, brown, and green, and impurities of chromium yield the green and red of alexandrite. Chrysoberyl is an extremely hard and durable mineral, inferior only to diamond and corundum. The name is a combination of the Greek word *chrysos,* meaning "golden," and the mineral beryl. It was thought to be a type of beryl until the late eighteenth century, when it was recognized as a distinct mineral.

Some chrysoberyl contains numerous parallel inclusions of fine, needle-like crystals, commonly of the mineral rutile (titanium oxide). If such stones are cut as cabochons in the proper orientation, light reflecting off the needles will concentrate in a bright band on the surface of the gem, perpendicular to the direction of the needles. Reminiscent of the vertical slit in the eyes of cats, this phenomenon, known as chatoyancy, is popularly called a cat's eye. The most prized cat's eyes are translucent, honey yellow to greenish brown in color, and have a sharp eye that appears to open and close as the angle of illumination changes. A variety of other gems can show a similar optical effect, but in the gem trade "cat's eye" is synonymous with chrysoberyl. Cat's eyes are considered by some to be a charm against evil spirits and have been a favored gem for engagement rings of the British royalty. They are especially fashionable in Japan and other Southeast Asian countries. The most important sources of cat's eye chrysoberyl are the gem gravels in Sri Lanka and pegmatite deposits in Brazil.

One of the most valuable and exotic gemstones is the variety of chrysoberyl known as alexandrite. Alexandrite is renowned for its dramatic color change, from deep cherry red under tungsten (incandescent) lights to brilliant green in daylight or under fluorescent lamps. It was named after Czar Alexander II, on whose birthday the gem allegedly was discovered in 1830 in the Ural Moun-

Left:
Alexandrite gems are known for their color change in response to different kinds of light. The three shown here, photographed under incandescent light, include a huge 65.08-carat gem from Sri Lanka, a 16.7-carat gem from Sri Lanka, and a 4.84-carat gem from Russia. Under fluorescent lights or in sunlight these stones appear green

Above:
Although better known for cat's eye and alexandrite varieties, chrysoberyl is also cut into such attractive gems as this 114-carat stone from Minas Gerais, Brazil

tains of Russia. Impurities of chromium atoms in chrysoberyl absorb light entering the stone such that nearly equal amounts of green and red light are transmitted to the eye. Tungsten lights radiate relatively strongly in the red portion of the spectrum, causing red to be dominant in the alexandrite. Sunlight and fluorescent light, on the other hand, are rich in green light, causing the gem to appear green. The green is also enhanced because the human eye is most sensitive to that color. Sri Lanka and Brazil are the leading producers of alexandrite, but gemstones that show the most dramatic color change have typically come from Russia. Alexandrite gems larger than a few carats are uncommon; one of the largest known is a 65.08-carat stone from Sri Lanka in the National Gem Collection.

Opposite:
With its exceptional size, honey color, and sharp band of light, the 58.2-carat Maharani Cat's Eye from Sri Lanka is one of the finest gems of its kind known

SPODUMENE

The name spodumene comes from a Greek word meaning "ash-colored," in reference to the gray color and dull, woody luster of typical spodumene crystals. In some places, however, spodumene is found as lustrous transparent pink or green crystals that can be cut into the gemstones known as kunzite and hiddenite, respectively.

Spodumene is lithium aluminum silicate and an important ore of the metal lithium. As the lightest metal, lithium is used in lightweight alloys; it is also used in batteries, and lithium compounds are used in antidepressant drugs, lubricants, and to color fireworks red. Spodumene is almost exclusively found in pegmatite deposits, sometimes in gigantic crystals. The largest mineral crystal ever found was a spodumene crystal in South Dakota that was 14.3 m (47 ft) long and weighed more than 90 tons. Gem-quality spodumene crystals, however, rarely are more than a few tens of centimeters in length. One of the finest gem-quality kunzite crystals known is in the National Gem and Mineral Collection; it is from Brazil and weighs about 7.5 kg (about 16.5 lb).

Kunzite gemstones are shades of violet and pink, caused by trace impurities of manganese. This spodumene gem was first discovered in Pala, California, in 1902, and was later named for the American gemologist George F. Kunz. Generally, the values of kunzite gems increase with the richness of their color. Kunzite gems must be cut relatively large to show a strong body color; small stones typically appear very light pink at best. Some kunzites fade in color upon exposure to light and can turn almost colorless. Consequently kunzite is known as an "evening stone," and should not be exposed for long periods to bright light, especially sunlight. The tendency of spodumene to cleave, or split along planes of weakness when struck, makes kunzite a challenging stone for gem cutters. This relative fragility makes it a gem more suited for use in pendants than rings or bracelets. Kunzite gemstones weighing several hundred carats are known, including a heart-shaped 880-carat gem in the National Gem Collection. The major sources of kunzite are Brazil, Afghanistan, California, and Madagascar.

Kunzite exhibits strong pleochroism: light traveling in each direction through a kunzite crystal interacts differently with the atomic structure, resulting in distinct colors. When viewed from different directions, the color

Right:

A 396.3-carat kunzite gem from Brazil and South Sea baroque pearls decorate a stunning necklace designed by Paloma Picasso in 1986 to celebrate the one hundredth anniversary of Tiffany & Company. Gift of Tiffany & Company, 1990

This delicate pink 880-carat heart-shaped kunzite gem comes from Brazil

of a kunzite crystal or gem can appear pale pink, nearly colorless to greenish, or intensely pink. Gem cutters must take this phenomenon into account so that the finished gem will show the deepest pink color.

In 1879, a vibrant green variety of spodumene was found associated with emerald in North Carolina, and was named hiddenite, after its discoverer W. E. Hidden. Hiddenite is the rarest spodumene gem, and the deep color of the crystals from North Carolina, caused by traces of chromium, has not been matched by any other locality. Brazil is the source of pale green to yellow spodumene, which is sometimes inappropriately marketed as hiddenite. Emerald green hiddenite has never been common, and cut stones larger than a couple of carats are extremely rare.

One of the largest gem-quality kunzite crystals known, weighing about 7.5 kg (16.4 lb), was found in Minas Gerais, Brazil. The three different views clearly show kunzite's pronounced pleochroism

The gem variety of zoisite known as tanzanite was first discovered in 1967 in Tanzania. This gem weighs 122.7 carats. A mirror reveals the gem's pleochroism

In 1967, violet blue crystals of the mineral zoisite were discovered in the foothills of Mount Kilimanjaro in Tanzania. Most zoisite is drab brown, gray, or green, and prior to 1967 the only zoisite (hydrous calcium aluminum silicate) used as an ornamental stone was the massive pink variety from Norway called thulite. But these new intensely colored crystals were extraordinarily beautiful and propelled zoisite into the ranks of the important gem minerals. Tiffany & Company marketed the new zoisite gems under the name of tanzanite, and since its discovery the gem has steadily increased in popularity.

The best tanzanite gemstones are deep sapphire blue with highlights of intense violet. Trace impurities of vanadium give tanzanite its color. It is common practice to heat-treat tanzanite crystals to create a more intense, uniform color. Tanzanite is strongly pleochroic, appearing intense blue, violet, or red depending on the direction through which the crystal or gem is viewed; consequently, the predominant hue of a tanzanite gem depends on the orientation in which it was cut. All tanzanite gemstones originate from the area where they were initially discovered in Tanzania, where they are mined from metamorphosed limestone.

5. Gems with Special Optical Properties

FELDSPAR GEMS:
MOONSTONE, SUNSTONE, AND LABRADORITE

The minerals in the feldspar family make up more than half of the Earth's rocky crust. Occasionally these common minerals form crystals that shimmer like the light of the moon or a rainbow on a soap bubble. Called iridescence, this phenomenon is caused by light scattering, or diffracting, off closely spaced layers in the feldspar crystals. The gems cut from these iridescent crystals are called moonstones, sunstones, and labradorite.

Page 110:
Moonstones are prized for their beautiful blue schiller (iridescent luster). This delicately carved 50.8-carat gem is from Sri Lanka

Left:
The golden sheen flashing off of a sunstone from Norway is caused by light reflecting off tiny flat crystals of the mineral hematite inside of the stone

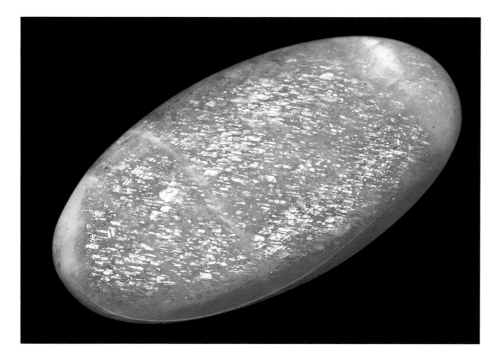

All of the minerals in the feldspar family have the same basic aluminum silicate atomic framework, combined with a variety of other elements, most commonly sodium, potassium, and calcium. They generally crystallize from cooling molten rock and are the major constituents of most igneous rocks such as granite and basalt. When most feldspar minerals form they contain both sodium and calcium or sodium and potassium atoms randomly mixed within the crystals. As the crystals cool, the atoms separate into alternating, microscopic sodium-, calcium-, or potassium-rich layers. If the thickness of these

Madagascar is the source of this rare orthoclase gem; at 250 carats it is one of the largest known

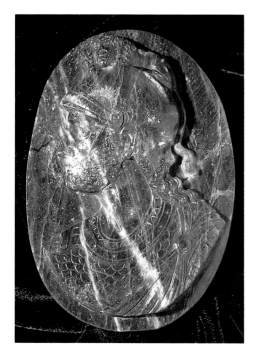

As the orientation of this labradorite carving is changed relative to the light, the iridescent colors flash off and on

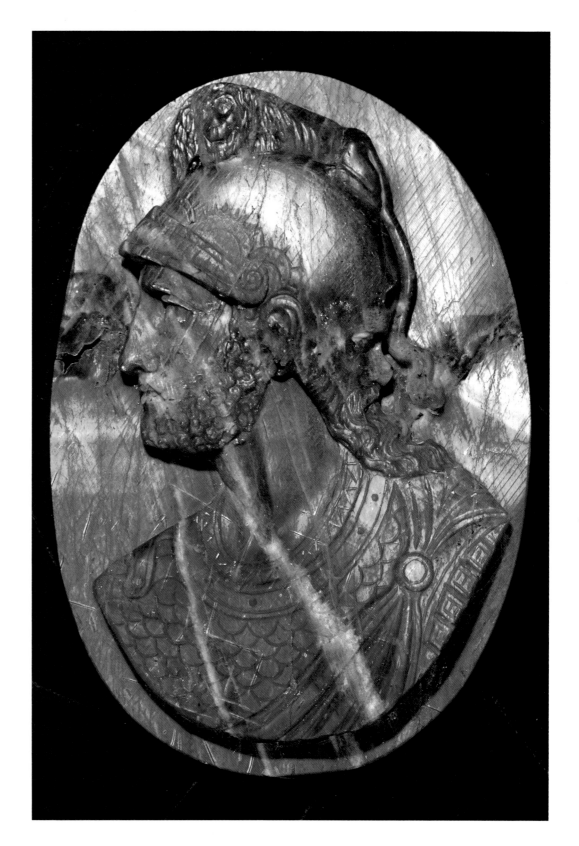

compositional layers is comparable to the wavelength of visible light, about 0.5 microns (0.00002 inches), the layers act like a diffraction grating, separating light into its component colors. A similar iridescence can be observed on compact disks (CDs) and some butterfly wings, where closely spaced grooves and layers within scales, respectively, diffract the light.

Moonstone is the most highly prized of the feldspar gems. Minute intergrowths of sodium- and potassium-rich feldspars (albite and orthoclase, respectively) are responsible for the soft white to bluish sheen, called adularescence, that appears to move across the surface of the stone as the viewing angle is changed. Flawless, clear, or translucent gems exhibiting a rich blue sheen are most valuable. Moonstones are typically cut as cabochons to best show off the effect, and they are sometimes carved. In India, moonstones have been considered sacred gems for many centuries and are popular there in jewelry. The finest moonstone gems come from Sri Lanka, Burma, and India.

Labradorite gets its colorful iridescence from light diffracting off closely spaced layers of calcium- and sodium-rich feldspar. As the stone is turned, intense flashes of blue, green, yellow, and red play across properly oriented surfaces. Top-quality material is typically cut as cabochons or used for carvings. The most important sources of iridescent labradorite are Labrador (for which it is named), Finland, and Madagascar.

Feldspars also yield a variety of other gem materials. Sunstones, typically the mineral oligoclase, exhibit a reddish to golden sheen, resulting from light reflecting off numerous tiny copper or hematite (iron oxide) flakes scattered within the stones. Most sunstone comes from Norway, Oregon, and Mexico. The blue-green variety of microcline, known as amazonite, is exclusively found in pegmatite deposits and is popular for use in beads and carvings. Rarely, orthoclase and labradorite occur in colorful, transparent crystals that can be cut as faceted stones. Madagascar is the most important source of facet-grade yellow orthoclase, and Oregon has produced a dazzling array of colorful labradorite gemstones.

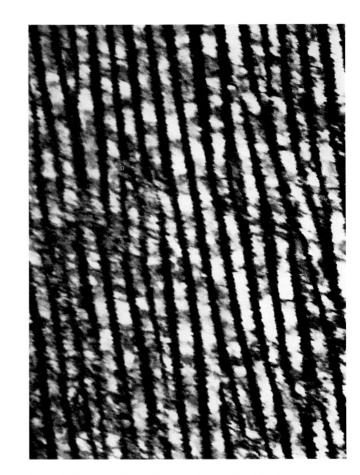

Labradorite crystallizes from molten rock at high temperatures (1,200 °C, or 2,190 °F). As it cools, its sodium and calcium atoms separate into layers, as seen in a transmission electron microscope image (magnification 58,000x). Light scattering off of the closely spaced layers produces colorful iridescence

OPAL

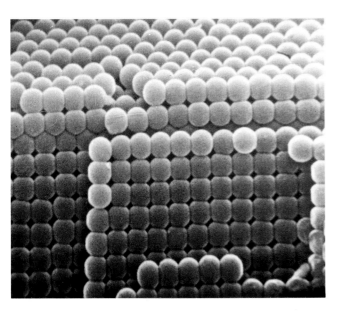

A scanning electron microscope reveals the orderly stacks of silica spheres in precious opal. The spheres are about 0.5 microns (0.00002 in) in diameter

The fiery play of colors in opal have intrigued people since ancient times. The Romans revered it as a symbol of hope and purity, and the Arabs believed opals fell from the skies in flashes of lightning. The name originates from the Sanskrit *upala*, meaning "precious stone."

Opal is a noncrystalline (amorphous), hydrated form of silica (silicon and oxygen), typically found in volcanic rocks or arid, sedimentary environments. Until late in the nineteenth century, the primary source of precious opal, including that used by the Romans, was mines near Dubník in present day Slovakia. Some opal was also mined in Central America by the Aztec. Opal was first discovered in Australia in 1872, and since then Australian precious opal has dominated the world markets.

The cause of the brilliant play of colors in opal was an enigma until relatively recently. Scanning electron microscope studies show that opals consist of transparent spheres of silica that are tightly packed. The voids, or spaces, among the spheres contain only air or water. In precious opal the silica spheres are of uniform size and are precisely stacked into an orderly three-dimensional arrangement (like the stacks of oranges at a grocery store). This regular arrangement of spheres—which resembles the arrangement of atoms in a crystal, except that the spheres are billions of times larger than atoms—acts as a diffraction grating, breaking visible white light into separate colors. Diffraction of light only occurs if the silica spheres are of the correct size (about 0.2 to 0.5 microns, or 0.000008 to 0.00002 in) and are precisely arranged. In lesser-quality opal the silica spheres are poorly shaped, of incorrect size, and/or not arranged in a regular pattern.

Opal is formed when silica slowly settles out of a dilute water solution. The spheres form as the water gradually evaporates. Opals can form only when an undisturbed space in a rock holds a clean solution of silica from which water is slowly removed over a period of thousands of years. In Andamooka, South Australia, opal formed about 40 m (131 ft) beneath the earth's surface in the free spaces among pebbles in a conglomerate, which is underlain by a layer of clay. Silica was leached from overlying rocks and carried down to the pebble layer. The downward movement of the water was stopped by the clay layer. The entire region dried out during several thousand years, allowing the silica

Opposite left:
Spectacular fire opals from
Mexico, ranging from 11 to
143 carats

Opposite right:
A magnificent 29.9-carat
faceted fire opal from
Jalisco, Mexico. Fire opal
gets its name from its
reddish orange body color
and may or may not show
flashes of other colors

Above:
An opal and gold necklace
designed by Louis Comfort
Tiffany about 1915–25 is ac-
cented with brilliant green
demantoid garnets from Russia.
The black opals are from
Lightning Ridge, Australia.
Gift of Ruth and Townsend
Treadway, 1974

Right:
Peacock brooch designed by
Harry Winston, Inc., featuring
a 32-carat black opal from
Lightning Ridge, Australia,
set off by sapphires, rubies,
emeralds, and diamonds. Gift
of Harry Winston, 1977

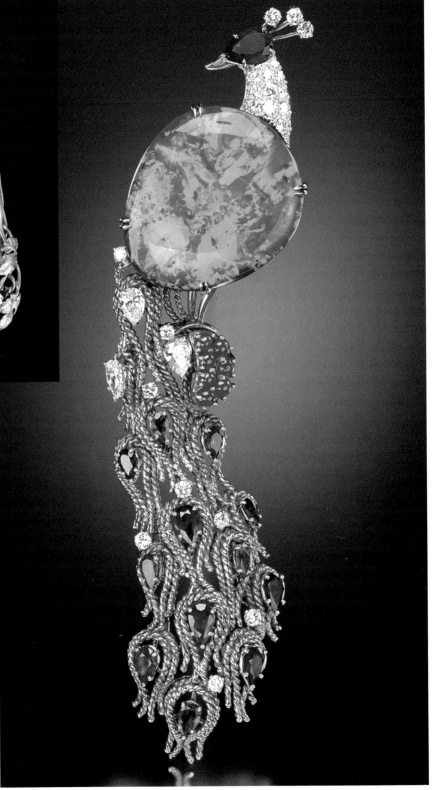

spheres to settle slowly out of solution and arrange themselves into an orderly three-dimensional formation. The spheres were cemented together by additional silica. Some opal is also found in volcanic rocks, where silica-bearing water solutions deposited silica in holes that formed as gas bubbles were trapped in cooling lava. Volcanic opal tends not to show the range and quality of fire as opals formed in sedimentary deposits. All precious opal is probably geologically young. It cannot withstand the heat and pressure associated with most long-term geological processes. Likewise exposure to weathering on the Earth's surface dries out opal, causing it to crack and turn opaque.

Opals are described according to their transparency and body color. White opals, translucent stones with a play of color against a white body color, are the most common. Opals with a vivid play of color and a black or other dark body color are called black opals. Top-quality black opals are highly prized but were not known until the discovery of the legendary Lightning Ridge opal field in Australia in 1903. Opals with a variety of intense colors, including red and violet, are generally the most expensive. Opals are typically cut as cabochons or polished free form to best show the play of colors.

Fire opals are transparent to semitransparent opals, resembling gelatin, with red, orange, or yellow body color, with or without play of color. The body color is caused by inclusions of iron oxides. They are also sometimes called Mexican opals because most of the best fire opals are found in Mexico, filling cavities in volcanic rock. Because of their transparency, fire opals are commonly faceted.

In 1829, Sir Walter Scott wrote the novel *Anne of Geierstein*, in which an opal was linked to tragedy, sparking a superstition that opals are unlucky. This unfortunate reputation was enhanced by the fact that it is a somewhat fragile gem. Because they are relatively soft and brittle, opals are easily scratched and chipped and are therefore more suitable for use in brooches and pendants than rings. As some opals dry out, especially if exposed to high temperatures, they tend to crack or craze. Opal's fragility makes it a challenging gem to cut and polish. Despite some of its weaknesses, opal's unique beauty makes it one of the most popular gems.

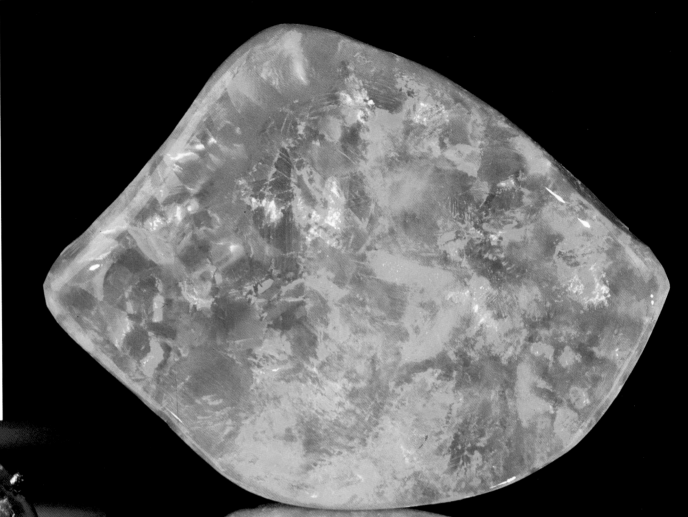

Right:

The Dark Jubilee Opal is a 318.4-carat free-form polished black opal from a mine in Coober Pedy, Australia. Coober Pedy means "a man in a hole" in a regional aboriginal language, and many miners do live in the underground excavations there. Gift of the Zale Corporation, 1980

Left:

The brilliant play of colors against a dark background make a superb black opal. This 26.9-carat stone is from Lightning Ridge, Australia. Gift of Mrs. Oliver B. James, 1970

119

STARS AND CAT'S EYES

Among the most intriguing members of the gem kingdom are those reflecting bright bands of light that form stars and cat's eyes. This optical phenomenon, called chatoyancy, which we encountered above in our discussion of chrysoberyl, is caused by light reflecting off of parallel bundles of tiny hollow tubes or fibrous crystals of another mineral inside the gemstone. When a properly oriented stone is cut into a rounded shape, called a cabochon, the reflected light is focused into bright bands on the surface that are perpendicular to each set of fibers or hollow tubes (similarly, a band of light can be observed perpendicular to the threads on a spool of thread held under a bright light). Gems, chrysoberyl being the classic example, showing a single bright band are called cat's eyes. Stars are formed when multiple bands intersect. Although many minerals can exhibit this effect, the most important star gems are sapphires and rubies.

Corundum crystals, including the gem varieties ruby and sapphire, typically form when clay-rich limestone is altered by heat and pressure. Pure corundum is aluminum oxide, but as the crystals grow they sometimes incorporate impurities of titanium that substitute for some of the aluminum atoms. Titanium atoms are slightly larger than aluminum atoms, but at the high temperatures at which the crystals form the size difference is not a problem. As the corundum crystals start to cool, however, they contract—the atoms move closer together, and the larger titanium atoms are squeezed. Eventually the titanium atoms are forced out of the corundum atomic framework, and they form their own crystals of the mineral rutile (titanium oxide) inside of the host corundum crystal. The threefold symmetry of the corundum atomic structure constrains the needlelike rutile crystals to align with equal probability in three directions, at 120° to each other. Light reflecting off of the three sets of parallel rutile needles yields the bands of light that intersect to form the six-rayed star. A similar sequence of events can play out in other minerals, but different atomic arrangements might cause the needles to align in only two directions, forming a four-rayed star, or in a single direction, yielding a cat's eye. Cat's eyes also can be caused by light reflecting off of parallel hollow tubes that formed inside of a crystal as it grew.

Stars and cat's eyes are best admired under sunlight or some other point light source. Multiple light sources each produce a star or cat's eye on the

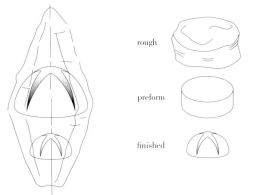

rough

preform

finished

The typical elongated shape of a sapphire crystal is sketched at left. The rutile crystal inclusions in some sapphires that give rise to the star effect always align perpendicular to the length of the crystal. Therefore, in order to exhibit a star, a gem must be cut from the crystal in the orientation shown

stone, giving it a fuzzy or unfocused look. The chatoyancy might disappear completely on a cloudy day or under fluorescent lights. The best star stones exhibit a well-centered star with all arms straight and of equal intensity, and a uniform and attractive body color. Large star sapphires and rubies, like cat's eye chrysoberyls, are rare and are commonly given names such as Star of Asia or Star of Bombay to heighten the intrigue and sense of the exotic surrounding many of these stones; more often than not, however, the monikers were bestowed by jewelers trying to make a sale.

Three of the world's most important star sapphires and rubies reside in the National Gem Collection: the 330-carat Star of Asia is acclaimed to be the finest and largest deep blue star sapphire; the 182-carat Star of Bombay once belonged to the silent-film actress Mary Pickford; and the 138.7-carat Rosser Reeves Star Ruby is by all accounts the largest fine star ruby.

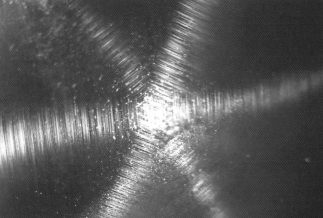

The extraordinary 330-carat Star of Asia (right) is one of the world's great star sapphires. It is renowned for its huge size, intense color, and sharp star. The gem is from Burma and is said to have once belonged to the maharaja of Jodhpur. A close-up view of the center of the star (above) reveals needlelike crystals of rutile oriented in three directions. Three bands of light reflecting off the rutile intersect to form the star

Left:
With its rich color and well-defined star, the 138.7-carat Rosser Reeves Star Ruby might be the largest and finest star ruby in the world. It is from Sri Lanka, but its early history is not known. When it was purchased by a gem dealer in London in the late 1950s, the ruby weighed 140 carats, but it was subsequently recut to center the star. Gift of Rosser Reeves, 1965

Below:
The 182-carat Star of Bombay sapphire is from Sri Lanka. It was given to movie star Mary Pickford—seen wearing it as a brooch in 1936 (below left)—by her husband, Douglas Fairbanks, and she bequeathed it to the National Gem Collection in 1981

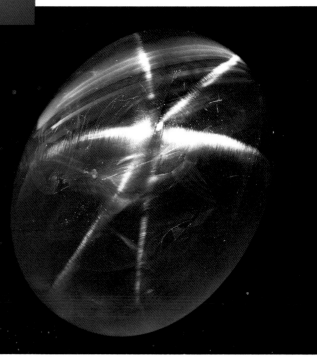

An Art Deco–style platinum necklace
designed by Marcus & Company features
a 60-carat sky blue star sapphire from
Sri Lanka in a diamond-studded setting

A black sapphire from Sri Lanka (70.8 carats) in a diamond and platinum ring exhibits a rare twelve-rayed star, probably caused by two sets of mineral inclusions, oriented thirty degrees from each other. Gift of Mrs. G. Burton Pearson, Jr.

Below:
The Burgundy Star Sapphire (50.4 carats) is from Sri Lanka and was part of the original Issac Lea Collection

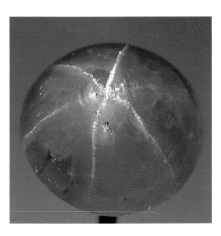

Many minerals can sometimes be cut as cat's eye gems. Clockwise from top: a 171.6 carat cat's eye chrysoberyl from Sri Lanka is one of the largest of its kind; a green elbaite gem (53.2 carats) from Brazil; a pink elbaite gem (17.5 carats) from California; a spectacular teal-colored elbaite gem (65.5 carats) from Brazil that forms its cat's eye as light reflects off of parallel grooves, or striations, on the back side of the stone that were on the original crystal surface; two scapolite gems from Burma, one a white stone (29.9 carats) and the other purple (3.3 carats); and a stunning golden beryl (43.5 carats) from Madagascar

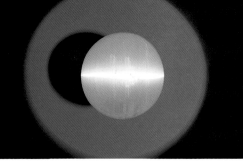

Light reflecting off numerous, tiny, parallel hollow tubes in a 54.88-carat aquamarine gem from Brazil causes the cat's eye

6. ORNAMENTAL STONES

JADE

Jade is a gem material most commonly associated with Asia, but the name comes from the Spanish *piedra de hijada,* meaning "stone of the loin," a term for green stones used by the native populations in Central America (the flat, smooth, and rounded cobbles resembled kidneys, and they were believed to have curative powers for certain kidney disorders). The Europeans extended the name to a similar green stone popularly used in China for carving. Not until the mid-nineteenth century was it realized that the name jade was being applied to two different minerals that have similar physical properties, nephrite and jadeite.

Jadeite is a sodium aluminum silicate, while nephrite is a variety of either tremolite or actinolite, calcium magnesium-iron aluminum silicates. Nephrite ranges from creamy white to green to almost black, depending upon the amount of iron in the mineral. Jadeite is white or green (iron), and rarely purple (manganese); sometimes all three colors are seen within a single piece. Translucent, emerald green jadeite, colored by chromium, is called imperial jade and is the most precious of all jade.

Jade is valued for its color and also its toughness, or resistance to breaking. The latter property has made jade useful historically for making weapons and tools, as well as for delicate carvings. The toughness results from the microscopic texture of the mineral crystals constituting jade. Nephrite crystals typically are fibrous and in jade are interwoven to produce a tough rock; jadeite occurs as blocky crystals that in jade tightly interlock, much like the pieces of a jigsaw puzzle. This difference in crystal texture can sometimes help distinguish between the two kinds of jade: nephrite commonly appears fibrous or silky, whereas jadeite has a more sugary or granular texture.

From as early as 1000 B.C. the Chinese were making weapons and ornaments from a green stone they called *yu,* now known as nephrite. Jadeite was not known in China until it was imported from Burma in the eighteenth century. Burma is still the most important source of fine jadeite, where it is found as rounded stream boulders and as pods in metamorphic rocks that have been altered at high pressure and relatively low temperature. Nephrite is more common than jadeite and also is found in metamorphic rocks; today the major sources are Russia, New Zealand, Taiwan, and British Columbia.

Page 126:
The Jade Dragon Vase stands 50 cm (19.7 in) tall and is carved of rare lavender jadeite from Burma. The carving is modern but of unknown origin. Gift of Mrs. Marjorie Merriweather Post

Jadeite is commonly found in Burma as rounded stream cobbles with a light-colored weathering rind. The stones are notched to assess the quality of the jadeite. The Chinese markings on this cobble (height 24.6 cm or 9.7 in) record dealer and inventory information

Three bowls carved from nephrite: the largest (height 9 cm or 3.5 in) is from British Columbia, Canada; the bowl on the left is from California; and the source of the nephrite used for the bowl on the right is unknown. Gifts of Mrs. Milton Turner (center) and Leonard J. Wilkinson (right)

Lapis Lazuli

With its intense deep blue color, lapis lazuli has been valued as an ornamental stone for more than six thousand years. The ancient Egyptians fashioned it into beads and carvings and powdered it for use as eye shadow. Historically, virtually all gem lapis lazuli was produced from a remote mountain valley in the Badakhshan region of Afghanistan. From there it was traded throughout the Middle East and Europe. During the Middle Ages, lapis lazuli was crushed to produce the precious paint pigment, ultramarine. The name lapis lazuli, derived from the Persian word *lazhward,* meaning "blue," did not come into use until the Middle Ages. The ancient Greeks and Romans referred to the blue stone as *sapphirus.*

Lapis lazuli is actually a rock composed of several minerals, primarily blue lazurite, with minor amounts of white calcite and pyrite. Lazurite is a complex sodium calcium aluminum silicate with variable amounts of sulfur and chlorine. The deep-blue color is caused by light interacting with the sulfur atoms. The source of the finest quality lapis lazuli is still Afghanistan, where it occurs as pods and seams in limestone that was altered by heat and pressure. Generally lesser-quality material is produced from Chile, where it was once mined by the Incas, and Russia.

Turquoise

Like lapis lazuli, turquoise has been used as a gem since ancient times, and might have been one of the first gem materials. It was mined by the Egyptians more than six thousand years ago, and also was prized for its sky blue color by the Aztecs and Incas, and later by Native Americans. It gets its name from the Old French *pierre Turquoise* or "stone of Turkey," in reference to the considerable Persian turquoise that was sold in Turkish markets.

Turquoise is a hydrous copper aluminum phosphate, and its blue color is due to the copper. Impurities of iron are responsible for greenish tones. Turquoise typically is found as compact masses consisting of microscopic crystals. It occurs in arid regions as veins and nodules in rocks that were deposited from water solutions that leached the necessary constituents from

Carved lapis lazuli (height 9.7 cm or 3.8 in) from Afghanistan. Gift of Leonard J. Wilkinson

Native Americans have long prized turquoise; here turquoise from the southwestern United States is set in a Navajo silver bracelet (height 11 cm or 4.3 in). Gift of Mr. and Mrs. M. Silverman

surrounding rocks. The finest turquoise, showing uniform, medium blue color, comes from mines near Nishapur, Iran, where it has been mined for more than three thousand years. Since World War II, however, production from Iran has declined and the United States, primarily Arizona and New Mexico, has been the principal source. Because turquoise is relatively soft and porous, it is commonly stabilized by impregnating it with plastic resins or silica.

The elegant box (diameter 14 cm or 5.5 in) created by Nikoli Medvedev is an outstanding example of intarsia, or stone inlay. Among the minerals represented in the box are malachite (green), rhodochrosite (pink), azurite (blue), sugilite (purple), and opal (white). Gift of Steven and Debra Daren, 1994

MALACHITE

Malachite is valued as a brilliant green ornamental stone, but also is an important ore of copper. It was used prior to 4000 B.C. by the Egyptians in decorative objects and as a cosmetic. The fine-grained masses of malachite used as an ornamental material commonly show light and dark colored bands that form bull's-eye and other intricate patterns. The intensities of the color layers correlate with the coarseness of the malachite crystals; layers consisting of larger crystals are darker green, while those made up of smaller crystals are pale green. Malachite is a hydrated copper carbonate that forms by chemical alteration of other copper ores. It sometimes forms as spectacular green stalactites and stalagmites, cross-sectional slices of which are prized for their intricate bull's-eye patterns. It commonly is found with its close relative, the deep blue mineral azurite. Malachite is primarily used in jewelry as beads and cabochons; it is also carved and used for inlays and veneers. Because it is a relatively soft mineral, malachite scratches easily and loses its polish with wear. The major source of gem malachite is Zaire.

Malachite grows in layers of tiny crystals, and its colors correlate with different crystal sizes: smaller crystals form light green bands and larger crystals make darker ones. This polished slice is from Zaire

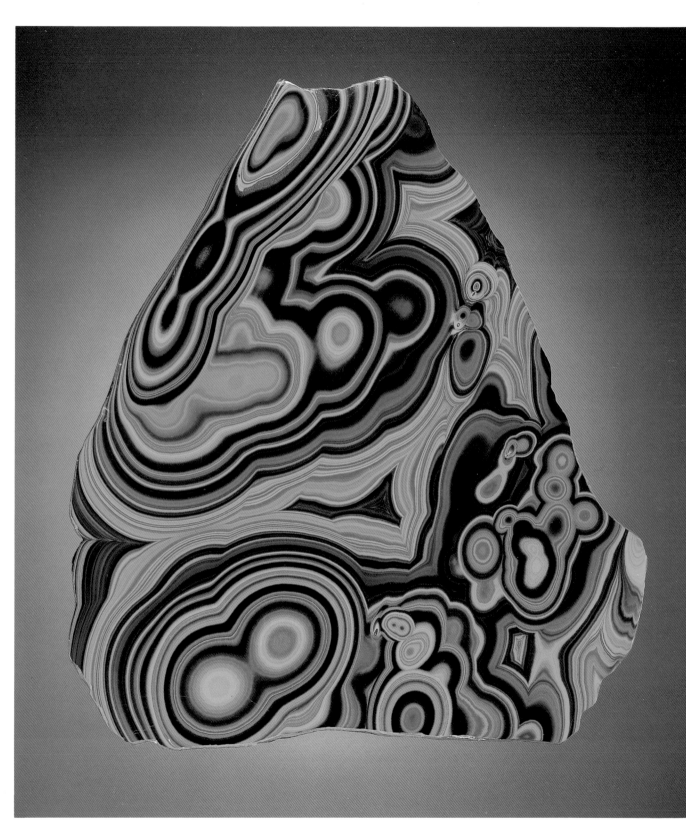

This amazing 3,965.3-carat blue fluorite gem from Hardin County, Illinois, might be the largest known gem of its kind. It was faceted by Art Grant. Gift of Harold and Doris Dibble

Because it is relatively soft and fragile, calcite is not normally an important gem mineral. This 1,800-carat calcite gem from Balmat, New York, is a spectacular display piece and a testament to the gem cutter's art, in this case that of Art Grant. It is probably the largest and finest faceted calcite in the world. Gift of Harold and Doris Dibble

APPENDIXES

RARE AND UNUSUAL GEMS

Below:
Center, a deep red rhodonite gem (4.9 carats) from Australia. Clockwise from top: a pale blue-green euclase gem (18.3 carats) from Brazil; a yellow titanite gem (14.4 carats) from Madagascar; a green, fan-shaped kornerupine gem (7.6 carats) from Madagascar; one of the largest-known brilliant blue benitoite gems (7.66 carat) from San Benito County, California, the sole source for specimens so deeply colored; a delicate yellow prehnite gem (8.5 carats) from Australia; and a golden-colored willemite gem (11.7 carats) from Franklin, New Jersey

Above:
Rhodochrosite (bottom center) is prized for its rose red color, but it is soft and gems, such as this 21.3-carat stone from South Africa, must be handled carefully. Sphalerite (top left) is the primary ore of zinc, but occasionally attractive crystals are found that can be cut into gems: this 87.9-carat orange-colored gem is from Spain. Completing the group are a light purple herderite gem (1.5 carats, bottom right) from Brazil; a yellow anglesite gem (18.6 carats, bottom left) from Morocco; and a golden yellow barite gem (37.5 carats, top right) from Italy

Right:

Colemanite (bottom right) is one of the main sources of boron, and although gems such as this 14.9-carat stone from Boron, California, are too soft to use in jewelry, they provide an interesting challenge for a skilled gem cutter. Sinhalite gems such as this huge 43.5 carat yellowish stone (top) from Sri Lanka were once thought to be a variety of peridot. They were recognized as a distinct mineral in 1952 and named for the major source, Sinhala, the Sanskrit name for Sri Lanka. Also shown are a 5.9-carat hambergite from Madagascar (left) and a light blue 2.98-carat jeremejevite from Namibia (bottom)

Left:

Center: a pale yellow stibiotantalite gem (7.3 carat) from Brazil. Clockwise from top: an exceptionally large deep red cuprite gem (203 carats) from Namibia; a colorless scheelite gem (37.04 carats) from California; an orange-red wulfenite gem (6.05 carats) from Arizona; a brilliant red zincite gem (20.1 carats); from Franklin, New Jersey; and a yellow scheelite gem (12.4 carats) from Arizona. Scheelite is the major ore of tungsten (used in light bulb filaments and special steel alloys), but occasionally crystals of scheelite are found that can be cut into gems

BIRTHSTONES

The custom of wearing a particular gem for the month in which one is born apparently originated in the sixteenth century in Germany or Poland, although at that time, the stones likely corresponded to the signs of the zodiac rather than the months of the year. The idea probably can be traced to the twelve Foundation Stones of the New Testament of the Bible, which in turn are based on the twelve precious stones of the High Priest's Breastplate, as listed in the Old Testament. There are various translations of the names of the stones in the Breastplate, complicated by the difficulty of translating the Hebrew words and the confused state of mineral nomenclature at the time. Consequently, several different lists of birthstones have appeared in different times and countries, various composites of which have been used in the United States over time. The twelve Breastplate stones are conventionally considered to be the following: (1) Carnelian, (2) Peridot, (3) Emerald, (4) Ruby, (5) Lapis lazuli, (6) Onyx, (7) Sapphire, (8) Agate, (9) Amethyst, (10) Topaz, (11) Beryl, (12) Jasper.

In 1952 the Jewelry Industry Council sponsored the birthstone list below, which supersedes previous lists adopted in 1912 by the American National Retail Jewelers' Association and in 1938 by the American Gem Society. When the new list is compared to the traditional birthstone list based on the biblical references it is apparent that a number of inexpensive stones, such as agate and lapis lazuli, have been replaced by more commercially lucrative gems, such as diamond and alexandrite. Despite the manipulations by the jewelry industry, the wearing of birthstones remains a pleasant custom that does convey meaning to many.

January	Garnet
February	Amethyst
March	Aquamarine or Bloodstone
April	Diamond
May	Emerald
June	Pearl, Moonstone, or Alexandrite
July	Ruby
August	Peridot or Sardonyx
September	Sapphire
October	Opal or Tourmaline
November	Topaz or Citrine
December	Turquoise or Zircon

GLOSSARY OF GEM-CUTTING TERMS

Baguette *A small step-cut gem with a long rectangular shape, commonly used as an accessory stone in jewelry.*

Baroque *An irregularly-shaped, rounded, polished gem. Usually used in reference to pearls, but also sometimes applied to other stones, such as emeralds.*

Brilliant cut *The cut most suitable for diamonds, giving the best balance of fire and brilliance. The standard brilliant cut consists of fifty-eight facets, thirty-three on the top (crown) and twenty-five on the bottom (pavilion). Variations of the brilliant cut include marquise, pear (pendaloque), and cushion shapes.*

Briolette *A droplet or barrel-shaped gem, typically diamond, covered with triangular or rectangular facets.*

Cabochon *A gem cut with a rounded top surface. This cut is used for translucent or opaque gems and to show off certain optical effects such as stars and cat's eyes.*

Crown *The top portion of a faceted gem.*

Culet *A small facet, parallel to the top (table) facet, sometimes added to the bottom (pavilion) of a brilliant-cut gem, usually to prevent chipping at the point where the pavilion facets meet.*

Cushion cut *A variation of the brilliant cut having a squarish shape with rounded corners.*

Dispersion *The ability of a gem to separate white light into its spectral colors; also known as fire.*

Emerald cut *See* step cut.

Girdle *The edge of a faceted stone between its top (crown) and lower (pavilion) portions.*

Marquise *A brilliant-cut stone with an outline that is boat-shaped.*

Pavé-set *A type of setting whereby small cut diamonds are inlaid so as to be flush with the surface of a piece of jewelry.*

Pavilion *The lower portion of a faceted gem.*

Rose cut *One of the earliest styles of faceting gems, with triangular facets on the upper portion only, the underside of the stone being flat. The name comes from the resemblance of the arrangement of facets to the petals of an opening rosebud. Traditionally, small diamonds and certain garnets have been cut in this style.*

Starburst cut *A variation of the brilliant cut having extra facets to add sparkle to the gem.*

Step cut *The cut most suitable for emeralds, aquamarines, and other intensely colored stones, sometimes called the emerald cut. This cutting style has a large top (table) facet surrounded by a series of steplike trapezoidal facets; the lower half of the stone (pavilion) has similarly arranged trapezoidal facets. Cut gems may be square, rectangular, triangular, kite-shaped, or other polygonal shapes. The large top facet allows abundant light to enter, bringing out the color.*

Table *The large facet at the top of a cut gem.*

Hardness Values for Important Gem Minerals

Mineral	Hardness
Beryl *(Emerald, Aquamarine, Heliodore, Morganite, Red Beryl, Green Beryl)*	7.5
Chrysoberyl *(Alexandrite, Cat's Eye)*	8.5
Corundum *(Ruby, Sapphire)*	9
Diamond	10
Feldspar family *(Moonstone, Sunstone, Labradorite, Orthoclase)*	6–6.5
Forsterite *(Peridot)*	6.5
Garnet family	6.5–7.5
Jadeite *(Jade)*	7
Lazurite *(Lapis Lazuli)*	5.5
Malachite	4
Nephrite *(Jade)*	6.5
Opal	5.5–6.5
Quartz	7
Rhodochrosite	4
Spinel	8
Spodumene *(Kunzite, Hiddenite)*	7
Topaz	8
Tourmaline family	7–7.5
Turquoise	5.5–6
Zircon	7–7.5
Zoisite *(Tanzanite)*	6

Hardness, or resistance to scratching, values are based on Moh's scale, having 1 as the softest and 10 the hardest. Gems harder than 7 resist scratching from normal dust; gems softer than 7 tend to lose luster after long wear. For comparative purposes, note that glass has a hardness value of 5.5, and fingernail tissue a hardness value of 2.5.

Diamond Grading

There are four primary factors that affect the value of diamond gems, the so-called four C's: cut, carat weight, color, and clarity.

The *cut* is the shape, proportions, and finish of a gem diamond. The proportions are the size and angle relationships among the facets on the different parts of the stone. Finish refers to the quality of the polish and the shape and placement of the facets. Cut affects both the weight yield from the rough and the brilliance and dispersion of the gem.

The standard unit of weight for diamonds and most other gems is the metric *carat*, equal to 0.200 grams. The more a gem weighs, the greater its value (although a heavier gem with poor cut, clarity, and color may, of course, be less valuable than a lighter specimen in which these qualities are superior).

Most diamonds have at least a trace of yellow, brown, or gray body *color*. A diamond's color is commonly graded using a system established by the Gemological Institute of America (GIA), which assesses the degree of yellow body color of a diamond on a scale ranging from "D" for diamonds without any trace of a yellow tint to "Z" for yellow stones. Generally diamonds with a grade of D, E, or F are referred to as colorless, G-J as near colorless, K-M as faint yellow, N-R as very light yellow, and S-Z as light yellow. Stones that are more intense yellow than "Z" are called fancy yellow. Diamonds might also be graded as fancy blue, green, red, pink, purple, and so forth.

The *clarity* of a diamond is a measure of how free it is from inclusions and other blemishes or flaws. Again, the most commonly used system for rating the clarity of diamonds is the one developed by the GIA:

Flawless (Fl): These diamonds show no blemishes or inclusions when examined under 10X magnification.

Internally Flawless (IF): The stones show no inclusions and only insignificant surface blemishes that can be removed by minor repolishing under 10X magnification.

Very Very Slightly Included (VVS$_1$ and VVS$_2$): VVS diamonds contain minute inclusions that are difficult to see under 10X magnification. In VVS$_1$ they are extremely difficult to see, or small and shallow enough to be removed by minor repolishing. In VVS$_2$ they are very difficult to see.

Very Slightly Included (VS$_1$ and VS$_2$): VS diamonds contain minor inclusions, such as mineral crystals, small "feathers," and distinct "clouds," ranging from difficult (VS$_1$) to somewhat easy (VS$_2$) to see.

Slightly Included (SI$_1$ and SI$_2$): SI diamonds contain noticeable inclusions that are easy (SI$_1$) or very easy (SI$_2$) to see under 10X magnification.

Imperfect (I$_1$, I$_2$, and I$_3$): I-grade diamonds contain obvious inclusions under 10X magnification that usually can be seen with the unaided eye.

Note: Gems are listed by carat weight/place of origin/catalogue number/donor. Further notations about individual stones appear at the end of certain entries. tw=total weight

Albite 42.62/Burma/G3311/
L. T. Chamberlain/cat's eye

Almandine 200.95/Idaho/G9874/star
174.15/Idaho/G3670/star
67.26/Idaho/G3560/L. T. Chamberlain
40.62/Madagascar/G2137/L. T. Chamberlain
25.73/Idaho/G3423/L. T. Chamberlain
5/Arizona/G2140/American Gem & Pearl
Company

Amblygonite 62.64/Brazil/G4079/
L. T. Chamberlain
57.79/Brazil/G8241/R. Zajicek
39.65/Brazil/G8058/H. I. Saul
19.70/Burma/G3562/W. A. Roebling

Andalusite 30.45/Brazil/G4939
28.24/Brazil/G3619/F. C. Kennedy
13.48/Brazil/G3364/L. T. Chamberlain

Andradite (demantoid) 10.40/Russia/G2175
4.13/Russia/G2150
3.36/Russia/G3627
3.14/Russia/G9868/J. A. Plugge

Anglesite 77.54/Namibia/G5706
70.22/Namibia/G9759/J. J. Trelawney
18.62/Morocco/G9837/L. T. Chamberlain
17.21/Morocco/G9750/L. T. Chamberlain

Apophyllite 15.39/India/G5395

Augelite 2.43/California/G8100/L. F. Stornelli

Barite 97.01/England/G8117/B. Roth
64.75/Colorado/G8062/H. I. Saul
60.68/England/G3349
37.50/Italy/G8633/A. A. Rasch

Benitoite 7.67/California/G3387/
W. A. Roebling
1.10/California/G4506/W. A. Roebling
0.95/California/G4174/L. T. Chamberlain

Beryl 1363.33/Brazil/G3916/green beryl
197.61/Brazil/G8807/E. L. Henning/
green beryl
103.61/Brazil/G8994/D. Warburton/
green beryl
99.07/Russia/G8450/R. W. F. Conway/
green beryl
81.85/Brazil/G8123/E. M. Hills/cat's eye/
green beryl
76.13/Brazil/G8993/D. Warburton/green beryl
19.79/Brazil/G3355/L. T. Chamberlain/
black star
14/Brazil/G6171/S. Thornton/black star

1.64/Utah/G9873/Diamond Consultants
International/red beryl

Beryl (aquamarine) 1000/Brazil/G3889/
Evyan Perfumes, Inc./"Most Precious"
914.38/Brazil/G3919
911/Brazil/G4348
577.85/Brazil/G3227/W. A. Roebling
311.83/Sri Lanka/G8982/C. Y. Hu
310.04/Brazil/G8973/J. P. Gills
263.51/Russia/G3606/Mrs. P. A. Neal
186.88/Brazil/G3683
184/Brazil/G6186/Mr. & Mrs. D. C. Harrold
126/Brazil/G4159/L. G. Erickson
120.95/Brazil/G8965/J. P. Gills
111.42/Idaho/G5005
100/place unknown/G9247/B. O. Hawk
88.95/Brazil/G9006/E. J. Gorny
82.45/Brazil/G8440/Dr. & Mrs.
L. W. Gaston
74.18/Sri Lanka/G7479/cat's eye
66.33/Maine/G2148
54.88/Brazil/G7760/Mr. & Mrs. P. M.
Klein/cat's eye
17.90/Kenya/G9035/Bay Shore Group
14.26/Connecticut/G0779
9.55/North Carolina/G0776/Isaac Lea Coll.
6.03/Zambia/G9872/L. T. Chamberlain

Beryl (emerald) 167.97/Colombia/G9775/
A. C. Mackay/Mackay emerald necklace
75.47/Colombia/G7719/J. A. Hooker/Hooker
emerald brooch
45/Colombia/G5113/C. H. Williams/
Inquisition necklace
37.82/Colombia/G4931/Mr. & Mrs. O. R.
Chalk/Chalk emerald ring
27.98/Colombia/G9207/Dr. & Mrs. B. T.
Swaykus
21.04/Colombia/G5024/M. M. Post/
Maximilian emerald ring
5.28/Colombia/G9122/L. Termin/trapiche
emerald
4.87/Colombia/G9135/L. Termin/trapiche
emerald
not weighed/Colombia/G5023/
M. M. Post/Indian emerald necklace

Beryl (goshenite) 72.65/Brazil/G8482/
P. B. Merkel
61.85/Brazil/G3366
41.69/Brazil/G9261/H. & D. Berman

Beryl (heliodore) 2054/Brazil/G3725
237.28/Brazil/G9991/M. E. Hartl
216/Brazil/G10066/Helene V. Rubin
133.46/Madagascar/G1977/L. T. Chamberlain
89.44/Brazil/G8986/C. O. Lowe
72.40/Brazil/G8886/Dr. & Mrs. R. L.
Bonsanti
61.92/place unknown/G9234/Dr. & Mrs.
L. J. Malone
59.54/Brazil/G8979/Mr. & Mrs. A. Kerckhoff

46.24/Madagascar/G2121/L. T. Chamberlain
44.10/Brazil/G8963/J. P. Gills
43.51/Madagascar /G3248/cat's eye
28.40/place unknown/G9262/H. & D.
Berman
8.78/Connecticut/G9959/S. Sweeney
3.77/Pennsylvania/G0792

Beryl (morganite) 331.41/Brazil/G7759/
Mr. & Mrs. P. M. Klein
235.50/Brazil/G3780/Mr. & Mrs. F. Ix
122.21/California/G1988/L. T. Chamberlain
113.20/California/G4286/L. T. Chamberlain
106.39/Brazil/G8806/E. L. Henning
93.83/Madagascar/G9224/J. J. Trelawney
82.82/Brazil/G5697/W. Mason
79.56/Brazil/G4190/W. A. Roebling
77.70/Maine/G9975/W. A. Roebling
56/Madagascar/G2223/W. A. Roebling
38.18/Mozambique/G8881/H. Bruder
14.25/California/G1876/L. T. Chamberlain

Beryllonite 5.01/Maine/G0423
3.86/Maine/G0424
3.34/Maine/G0425

Boracite 1.08/Germany/G9809/V. Yount

Brazilianite 41.89/Brazil/G3083/
L. T. Chamberlain
16.64/Brazil/G3788/W. A. Roebling

Calcite 1800/New York/G10046/
H. & D. Dibble
475.38/Russia/G8126/C. Krotki
326.66/Russia/G9570/I. Putterman
150.61/Mexico/G8442/J. E. Klijanowicz
122.32/Mexico/G8869/P. Van der Voorn
110.66/Africa/G8899/C. Entenmann
75.70/Mexico/G4583/W. A. Roebling
70.23/Mexico/G7910/N. R. Leader
52.26/New York/G9892/L. T. Chamberlain
45.80/Mexico/G3305
3.97/Spain/G4176/L. T. Chamberlain/
cobaltian

Cassiterite 9.95/Bolivia/G3250

Celestite 16.76/Madagascar/G8924/C.
Entenmann

Cerussite 339.85/Namibia/G8889/
S. L. Leventhal
252.49/Namibia/G8833/V. H. Hansford
179.19/Zambia/G9048/Bay Shore Group
75.10/Namibia/G8673/C. DeBoer
6.66/Namibia/G3792/
W. A. Roebling/cat's eye

Chrysoberyl 171.50/Sri Lanka/G3924/
cat's eye
120.46/Sri Lanka/G3001/W. A. Roebling
114.25/Brazil/G4905

58.19/Sri Lanka/G3642/Maharani cat's eye
54.73/Sri Lanka/G9574/M. L. Briggs/
cat's eye
46.31/Brazil/G1923/L. T. Chamberlain
13.79/Brazil/G2250/W. A. Roebling
6.65/place unknown/G3680/
Mrs. E. Ware/star
not weighed/Sri Lanka/G9566/
E. Scheffres/cat's eye

Chrysoberyl (alexandrite) 65.08/Sri
Lanka/G2042/L. T. Chamberlain
48.20/Sri Lanka/G9758/Meltzer, Meltzer,
Avick, Kaufman
16.69/Sri Lanka/G3407/W. A. Roebling
4.84/Russia/G10065/J. P. Gorrell
3.49/Russia/G3120/L. T. Chamberlain

Colemanite 23.14/California/G8061/
H. I. Saul
14.85/California/G4941/L. T. Chamberlain

Cordierite 15.55/Sri Lanka/G3882
11.03/place unknown/G9865/
D. J. Duke/cat's eye
10.23/Sri Lanka/G3580
9.46/Sri Lanka/G3881

Corundum (ruby) 138.72/Sri Lanka/
G4257/R. Reeves II/ Rosser Reeves star
ruby
5.65/Thailand/G8479/Mrs. W. C. Hazen
4.94/Thailand/G2086
3.89/Thailand/G8481/Mr. & Mrs.
E. J. Slattery
3.76/Thailand/G9418/P. D. Cerami &
L. T. Jones
3.56/Thailand/G9419/P. D. Cerami &
L. T. Jones
3.32/Thailand/G9215/Mr. & Mrs. R. L. Hall
3.09/Thailand/G9088/E. Aaron
3/Thailand/G8484/D. Feriozi
0.89/North Carolina/G0195
60tw/Burma/G5020/Anonymous/
ruby and diamond bracelet

Corundum (sapphire) 422.99/Sri Lanka/
G3703/Mrs. J. Logan/Logan sapphire
329.70/Burma/G3688/Star of Asia
287.32/Sri Lanka/G2231/W. F. Ingram/
Star of Artaban
181.82/Sri Lanka/G8845/M. P. Rogers/
Star of Bombay
98.57/Sri Lanka/G4753/Countess M.
Bismarck/Bismarck sapphire necklace
92.60/Burma/G3549/yellow
70.79/Sri Lanka/G9219/
Mrs. G. B. Pearson, Jr./black star
67.10/Thailand/G4375/
L. T. Chamberlain/black star sapphire
62.49/Sri Lanka/G9285/J. A. Thiel/yellow
62.03/Australia/G4657/A. R. Cutter/
black star sapphire

60/Sri Lanka/G8887/Mrs. W. C. Crane/
   star sapphire necklace
55/Sri Lanka/G7722/W. B. Berry/blue
50.71/Sri Lanka/G8500/W. R.
   Persons/yellow
50.41/Sri Lanka/G0173/Isaac Lea Coll./
   burgundy star sapphire
42.19/Sri Lanka/G4371/
   Mr. & Mrs. J. H. Clark/purple
39.77/Sri Lanka/G0174/
   Isaac Lea Coll./purple star
38.63/Australia/G4924/A. R. Cutter/
   black star
36.10/Sri Lanka/G8839/V. K. Kampf/
   blue star
35.40/Sri Lanka/G2147/yellow
31.06/Sri Lanka/G4357/
   Mr. & Mrs. J. H. Clark/pink-orange
30/Sri Lanka/G10069/C. T. P. Jenkins
29.11/Sri Lanka/G8952/J. P. Gills/purple
27.42/Sri Lanka/G4370/
   Mr. & Mrs. J. H. Clark/purple
25.28/Sri Lanka/G2016/
   L. T. Chamberlain/colorless
22.37/Sri Lanka/G3875/
   L. T. Chamberlain/yellow
19.90/Sri Lanka/G4372/
   Mr. & Mrs. J. H. Clark/purple
16.80/Burma/G2172/
   L. T. Chamberlain/green
15.82/place unknown/G9713/
   W. R. Persons/blue
15.73/Sri Lanka/G3581/blue
15.16/place unknown/G3106/
   L. T. Chamberlain/orange-pink
12.82/Sri Lanka/G4373/
   Mr. & Mrs. J. H. Clark/pink
11.58/Australia/G9818/
   E. P. Henderson/green
10.70/Tanzania/G8870/J. S. Hayward/
   purple
10.28/place unknown/G9808/
   Mr. & Mrs. J. A. Plugge/pink
10.20/Montana/G7707/blue
8.12/Sri Lanka/G8503/
   The Burstein family/blue
6.84/Sri Lanka/G0198/Isaac Lea Coll.
4.19/Sri Lanka/G0197/L. T. Chamberlain
2.35/Montana/G8619/B. E. Dahrling/
   blue
1.91, 1.99, 2.25/Montana/G3631/
   Kazanjian Brothers/blue-purple
1.75/Sri Lanka/G9217/A. E. Wicks/pink
195tw/Sri Lanka/G8044/
   E. A. Hall/Hall sapphire necklace

Crocoite 5.72/Australia/G8139/
   C. DeBoer

Cuprite 203.88/Namibia/G8122/
   T. E. Whiteley
172/Namibia/G5705

Danburite 33.70/Russia/G8813/W. Pinch
26.12/Madagascar/G9757/L. T. Chamberlain
18.46/Burma/G3345/L. T. Chamberlain
7.85/Japan/G3081/Isaac Lea Coll.

Datolite 23.65/Norway/G10017/
   L. T. Chamberlain
5.42/Massachusetts/G3876

Diamond 127.01/South Africa/G3898/Por-
   tuguese diamond
67.89/South Africa/G7101/Mr. & Mrs. L.
   Wilkinson/Victoria Transvaal necklace
61.12/place unknown/G10053/
   J. A. Hooker/Hooker yellow ring
45.52/India/G3551/H. Winston, Inc./
   Hope diamond
36.73/place unknown/G9997/
   L. M. Thompson/cognac brooch
30.62/South Africa/G4873/M. M. Post/
   Blue Heart ring
28.29/South Africa/G4220/A. C. Riggs/
   marquise ring
25.28, 25.30/place unknown/G10052/
   J. A. Hooker/Hooker yellow earrings
22/place unknown/G7107/Mr. & Mrs. L.
   Wilkinson/pale yellow ring
19.12, 20.46/place unknown/G9998/
   L. M. Thompson/cognac earrings
18.29/South Africa/G3406/
   Shepard diamond/yellow
16.72/South Africa/G7114/
   Mrs. G. B. Pearson, Jr.
15.79/place unknown/G9578/
   Mrs. J. S. Niedringhaus/champagne
14.25, 20.34/place unknown/G5018/Mrs. E.
   C. Barzin/Marie Antoinette earrings
12/place unknown/G4668/
   Mrs. O. B. James/Canary diamond
8.97/South Africa/G8043
8.52/place unknown/G9864/
   C. M. Bolin/Sherman diamond
7.79/Zaire/G5274/Humphrey diamond
5.32/place unknown/G8503/
   The Burstein family
5.03/place unknown/G9871/
   S. S. DeYoung/red
3.44/place unknown/G7105/Mr. & Mrs.
   L. Wilkinson/green irradiated
2.86/Tanzania/G3772/S. S. DeYoung/pink
2.31/Arkansas/G9920
700tw/place unknown/G5021/
   M. M. Post/Marie Louise Diadem
263tw/Brazil/G5019/M. M. Post/
   Napoleon necklace
244.10tw/place unknown/G10051/
   J. A. Hooker/Hooker yellow necklace
131.43tw/place unknown/G8045/
   L. A. Hazen/Hazen necklace
61.30tw/place unknown/G7106/Mr. & Mrs.
   L. Wilkinson/Wilkinson brooch
10.64tw/place unknown/G9999/
   Global Diamonds Inc./diamond alphabet

Diaspore 27.75/Turkey/G9286/M. Morris
10.63/Turkey/G9267/A. A. Rasch

Diopside 132.50/India/G3977/
   Adris Oriental Gem & Art Corp./star
19.18/Madagascar/G4504/W. A. Roebling
8.66/New York/G4936/L. T. Chamberlain
6.91/Italy/G3634

4.76/New York/G9972/G. Robinson
3.05/Russia/G8922/C. Entenmann/chrome
1.60/Finland/G3693/chrome

Ekanite 21.54/Sri Lanka/G9891/
   L. T. Chamberlain

Elbaite 258.07/Brazil/G9284/J. P. Young/
   cat's eye
216.82/Mozambique/G8945/J. P. Gills
212/Brazil/G8607/E. J. Cunningham/bicolored
172.65/Mozambique/G3590/W. A. Roebling
151.20/Maine/G5108
131.09/Mozambique/G8948/P. J. Peltier
122.89/Mozambique/G3575/W. A. Roebling
117.62/Brazil/G4349
110.99/place unknown/G9906/C. R. Read, Sr.
109.64/Brazil/G4197
102.38/Mozambique/G8946/P. J. Peltier
80.95/Mozambique/G9027/Bay Shore Group
76/Brazil/G3599/L. T. Chamberlain/cat's eye
71.07/Afghanistan/G9717
65.38/Brazil/G5700/Mr. & Mrs. H. Stuart/
   cat's eye
60/Brazil/G3410/W. A. Roebling
58.46/Maine/G1108/L. T. Chamberlain
53.20/Brazil/G3119/L. T. Chamberlain/cat's eye
53.10/Brazil/G8953/J. P. Gills
52.75/Mozambique/G9023/Bay Shore Group
52.67/Mozambique/G8485/R. W. Brink
48.66/Maine/G8980/Mr. & Mrs. A. F. Kerckhoff
48.03/California/G3363/bicolored
45.96/Afghanistan/G5015
44.18/Maine/G9714/bicolored
41.65/Brazil/G2251/W. A. Roebling
40.34/Tanzania/G4935/L. T. Chamberlain
40.25/Madagascar/G4081/
   L. T. Chamberlain/tricolored
40.21/Brazil/G2097
37.01/Brazil/G8955/J. P. Gills/tricolored
35.19/Maine/G8068/H. I. Saul
34.59/Brazil/G9977/bicolored
34.32/Brazil/G2253/W. A. Roebling
31.89/Afghanistan/G9147/achroite
31.65/Brazil/G3414/W. A. Roebling
31.30/Maine /G9754/N. Yedlin
31.25/Brazil/G3416/W. A. Roebling
30.44/Maine/G9860
28.60/Afghanistan/G9718
25.47/Brazil/G3298/W. A. Roebling/indicolite
21.09/Maine/G4621/L. T. Chamberlain
20.36/Madagascar/G2032/L. T. Chamberlain
18.04/Brazil/G2142/L. T. Chamberlain
17.94/South Africa/G2095
17.66/Italy/G3368
17/Maine/G1955/L. T. Chamberlain
8.57/Kenya/G8914/C. Entenmann
8.10/Afghanistan/G5008
6.69/Brazil/G9964/Blue Paraiba
6.50/Russia/G4507/W. A. Roebling
3.03, 3.23/Zambia/G9970/
   W. A. Roebling/yellow

Elbaite (rubellite) 116.20/California/G8110/
   I. Putterman
110.80/China/G3173/W. A. Roebling
103.92/Mozambique/G3256/L. T. Chamberlain

100.39/California/G8137/B. E. Dahrling
62.42/Brazil/G3411/W. A. Roebling
55.83/California/G8901/C. Entenmann
50.50/Brazil/G4160/L. G. Erickson/with
   diamond
47.71/California/G9024/Bay Shore Group
37.84/California/G8455/
   Dr. & Mrs. C. C. Chiu
35.28/Brazil/G2254/W. A. Roebling
29.98/Madagascar/G3409/W. A. Roebling
28.20/place unknown/G4358/
   Mr. & Mrs. J. H. Clark
24/California /G8900/C. Entenmann
21.15/Brazil/G9420/P. D. Cerami &
   L. T. Jones
19.16/Brazil/G2143
18.75/Madagascar/G4196/L. T. Chamberlain
18.39/Maine/G1109/Isaac Lea Coll.
17.50/California/G3786/
   L. T. Chamberlain/cat's eye
15.91/Madagascar/G2135

Enstatite 10.96/Sri Lanka/G3638
8.07/Sri Lanka/G2294/W. A. Roebling
5.78/Sri Lanka/G9769/L. T. Chamberlain

Epidote 3.92/Austria/G0579

Euclase 18.30/Brazil/G8834/
   Dr. & Mrs. C. C. Chiu
12.54/Brazil/G3214/W. A. Roebling
8.91/Brazil/G2181/L. T. Chamberlain
7.66/Brazil/G8453/Dr. & Mrs. C. C. Chiu

Ferroaxinite 23.59/Mexico/G4289/
   W. A. Roebling
9.27/Mexico/G3773/L. T. Chamberlain

Fluorapatite 140.95/Kenya/G8981/
   Mr. & Mrs. A. F. Kerckhoff
51.35/Mexico/G4943
47.50/Brazil/G9726
46.22/Brazil/G7726/P. Bagchi/cat's eye
30.98/Kenya /G8459/Dr. & Mrs. C. C. Chiu
29/Mexico/G3594
28.77/Burma/G3247/L. T. Chamberlain
14.66/Burma/G3720/W. A. Roebling
9.04/Canada/G3122/W. A. Roebling
8.82/Sri Lanka/G3639
2.34/Brazil/G8826
1.96/Madagascar/G9974/L. T. Chamberlain

Fluorite 3965.35/Illinois/G10031/
   H. & D. Dibble
846.43/Tennessee/G8436/R. Bideaux
729.26/Colombia/G8105/B. N. Bhat
611.47/Australia/G8849/A. G. H. Bing
492.15/Korea/G7905/J. F. Gratz, Jr.
354.39/Korea/G7907/J. F. Gratz, Jr.
353.79/Illinois/G3877
348.26/Korea/G7906/J. F. Gratz, Jr.
273.73/South Africa/G8876/Mr. & Mrs. I.
   Putterman
237.2/New Hampshire/G10059/R. L. Borofsky
234.59/Tanzania/G8094/B. H. Caldwell, Jr.
229.27/New Hampshire/G8096/
   B. H. Caldwell, Jr.

203.41/England/G8108/P. Bagchi
124.50/New Hampshire/G3294
118.87/Illinois/G8101/B. N. Bhat
118.74/England/G8098/B. H. Caldwell, Jr.
118.08/New Hampshire/G8425/S. Gott
117/Africa/G2153
111.23/Illinois/G4270
107.84/Mexico/G7837
105.36/Spain/G8095/B. H. Caldwell, Jr.
105.28/Colombia/G8089/B. H. Caldwell, Jr.
104.31/Illinois/G4269
99.82/South Africa/G8106/K. Kawaoka
96.57/South Africa/G8424/S. Gott
86.92/Illinois/G4875
84.66/Tennessee/G8971/J. P. Gills
83.02/Korea/G8140/D. J. Tepper
79.96/Illinois/G8898/C. Entenmann
69.78/Illinois/G8911/C. Entenmann
69.31/Colombia/G8103/B. N. Bhat
57.78/South Africa/G4934/W. A. Roebling
52.77/Namibia/G7911/N. R. Leader
52.74/Canada/G8092/B. H. Caldwell, Jr.
49.39/Colombia/G4945
48.41/Switzerland/G8810
46.91/Illinois/G5394
42.52/England/G8426/S. Gott
39.69/England/G7908/J. F. Gratz, Jr.
32.67/Illinois/G3626
24.20/New York/G8104/B. N. Bhat
17.50/Illinois/G3635
17.24/Illinois/G7909/J. F. Gratz, Jr.
12.93/Switzerland/G4434/F. A. Canfield

Forsterite (peridot) 311.78/Egypt/G3398/
W. A. Roebling
286.63/Burma/G3705
122.67/Burma/G8964/J. P. Gills
103.23/Burma/G7832/D. B. Dubin
34.65/Arizona/G9919/necklace
22.90/Arizona/G3620
18.13/Pakistan/G10060
11.95/Burma/G3347/L. T. Chamberlain/star
8.93/Arizona/G1925/L. T. Chamberlain
4.08/Norway/G9982/G. F. Imes & J. Parsons
3.07/Antarctica/G9712/E. J. Zeller &
G. A. M. Dreschoff

Grossular 30.07/Sri Lanka/G10068/
B. J. Whittle
29/Tanzania/G8582/N. H. Stavisky/tsavorite
9.85/Tanzania/G9663/M. E. Hartl/tsavorite
9.18/Sri Lanka/G2246/W. A. Roebling
8.87/Canada/G9836/L. T. Chamberlain
7.08/Tanzania/G8878/Mr. & Mrs.
M. Greenman/tsavorite
5.20/Kenya/G8616/B. E. Dahrling/tsavorite
2.59/Canada/G9154/L. T. Chamberlain
30.79tw/Tanzania/G9000/B. O. Hawk/
tsavorite necklace

Hambergite 40.23/Madagascar/G9172/
T. Whiteley
5.93/Madagascar/G8817
2.90/Madagascar/G7838
2.60/Madagascar/G7840

Hauyne 0.32/Germany/G9771/
L. T. Chamberlain

Herderite 5.90/Brazil/G4948/
Mr. & Mrs. B. Berman
1.49/Brazil/G8419/W. Pinch

Jeremejevite 2.98/Namibia/G8456/
Dr. & Mrs. C. C. Chiu
1.66/Namibia/G8677/C. DeBoer

Kornerupine 21.58/Sri Lanka/G3706/
L. T. Chamberlain
10.06/Madagascar/G9761
7.58/Madagascar/G3782
1.02/Kenya/G8461/Dr. & Mrs. C. C. Chiu/
chromian

Kyanite 36.57/Brazil/G8499/S. Miller
28.40/Brazil/G9762
10.65/Brazil/G3557/L. T. Chamberlain
9.05/Brazil/G3558/L. T. Chamberlain
4.85/Tanzania/G4508/L. T. Chamberlain
3.73/North Carolina/G0564/D. A. Bowman

Labradorite 30/Idaho/G5703/
L. T. Chamberlain
11.49/Oregon/G9611/W. E. Chaikin, T. G.
Deemer, L. A. Smith, R. Chaikin
11.07/Utah/G3121
7.73/Oregon/G9610/W. E. Chaikin, T. G.
Deemer, L. A. Smith, R. Chaikin
7.45/Oregon/G9960/C. L. Johnson/sunstone
7/Oregon/G9659/W. E. Chaikin, T. G. Deemer,
L. A. Smith, R. Chaikin/sunstone
5.28/Oregon/G9608/W. E. Chaikin,
T. G. Deemer, L. A. Smith, R. Chaikin
4.07/Oregon/G9609/W. E. Chaikin, T. G.
Deemer, L. A. Smith, R. Chaikin
1.71/Oregon/G2114/L. T. Chamberlain
3.23tw/Oregon/G9992/C. L. Johnson

Liddicoatite 10.33/Brazil/G9957/
L. T. Chamberlain

Legrandite 3.35/Mexico/G9218/C. DeBoer

Magnesite 389.28/Brazil/G8882/
W. H. Mosmann
93.47/Brazil/G8873/C. Krotki

Microlite 3.66/Virginia/G3588

Natrolite 9.31/New Jersey/G5111
7.90/New Jersey/G5116
3.68/California/G7912/N. R. Leader

Oligoclase 6.04/North Carolina/G0404

Opal 354.14/Nevada/G3969/
W. A. Roebling
318.38/Australia/G8827/Zale Corporation/
Black Jubilee opal
217.28/Australia/G9264/J. P. Gills
185.38/Honduras/G9853/M. Martin
174.90/Australia/G8469/J. P. Gills
155/Australia/G3285/W. A. Roebling
145.81/Mexico/G9016/Bay Shore Group
143.17/Mexico/G3968
92.70/Mexico/G8445/M. Braiman/hyalite
92.06/Australia/G8950/J. & J. S. Pollon

83.02/Australia/G3300/W. A. Roebling
62.80/Mexico/G9107/E. Aaron
58.75/Australia/G3960/W. A. Roebling
55.87/Mexico/G2240/W. A. Roebling
54.25/Australia/G3962/W. A. Roebling
48.32/Brazil/G9268
44.20/Australia/G8829/W. R. Persons
42.91/Australia/G3284/W. A. Roebling
38.53/Brazil/G3637
35.20/Brazil /G8431/R. R. Firth
32/Australia/G7987/H. Winston, Inc./
Peacock brooch
30.08/Australia/G3405/W. A. Roebling
29.86/Mexico/G5393
29.64/Slovakia/G2045/L. T. Chamberlain
28.21/Brazil/G9763
26.90/Australia/G4664/Mrs. O. B. James/
black opal ring
26.36/Mexico/G3571
24.09/Australia/G1897/L. T. Chamberlain
21.78/Mexico/G2028/L. T. Chamberlain
21.59/Mexico/G2106/L. T. Chamberlain
21.37/Mexico/G2111/L. T. Chamberlain
19.99/Mexico/G0461
18.87/Brazil/G3228/L. T. Chamberlain
14.90/Mexico/G2103/L. T. Chamberlain
14.53/Mexico/G1072/L. T. Chamberlain
14.46/Mexico/G3963/L. T. Chamberlain
11.81/Mexico/G2112/L. T. Chamberlain
11.54/Mexico/G3886/F. A. Lewis
11.24/Mexico/G3964/L. T. Chamberlain
11/Mexico/G3959
10.86/Australia/G3404/W. A. Roebling
10.80/Mexico/G4564
10.63/Mexico/G2289/H. M. Paskow
not weighed/Australia/G5120/
Mrs. F. R. Downs, Jr. & Mrs. R. O.
Abbott, Jr./Tiffany necklace

Orthoclase 249.45/Madagascar/G3878
150.18/Sri Lanka/G7834/Allan L. Burr/
moonstone
126.42/Madagascar/G8610/B. E. Dahrling
122.13/Sri Lanka/G7728/P. Bagchi/moonstone
119/Sri Lanka/G3884/cat's eye
104.50/Sri Lanka/G3883/cat's eye
60.97/Madagascar/G1838/L. T. Chamberlain
50.77/Sri Lanka/G2104/L. T. Chamberlain/
moonstone
45.54/Sri Lanka/G0409/moonstone
25.85/Sri Lanka/G3579/
L. T. Chamberlain/cat's eye
24.38/Sri Lanka/G4134/
L. T. Chamberlain/moonstone
22.65/Sri Lanka/G3578
14.8/Austria/G0417/moonstone
4.75/Burma/G8821/moonstone

Parisite 10.79/Colombia/G9856/
L. T. Chamberlain

Petalite 126.98/Brazil/G8809
55/Namibia/G4222/L. T. Chamberlain

Phenakite 58.90/Sri Lanka/G9866/
L. T. Chamberlain/cat's eye
21.85/Brazil/G4938
17.85/Russia/G3739

Phosphophyllite 26.89/Bolivia/G7848/S.
Korfmacher

Pollucite 8.50/Maine/G2056/
L. T. Chamberlain

Prehnite 8.51/Australia/G8923/
C. Entenmann

Pyrope 108.69/place unknown/G8975/
G. P. Mihok
74.26/Tanzania/G4806/H. Saul/rhodolite
63.34/Tanzania/G8447/D. M. DeLeo/
rhodolite
40.80/Tanzania/G9208/
L. R. Klepper
33.87/Tanzania/G9409/
R. J. Studders/rhodolite
27.87/Kenya/G9573/
E. J. Cunningham
22.06/Tanzania/G4080/
L. T. Chamberlain/rhodolite
16.54/North Carolina/G4361/
Mr. & Mrs. J. H. Clark/rhodolite
6.43/North Carolina/G0460/
Isaac Lea Coll. /rhodolite
not weighed/Czech Republic/G2164-2/
M. & A. Herdlicha/hairpin

Quartz 7478/Brazil/G3957/faceted egg
2670/Brazil/G8978/Mr. S. Cardinal/rutilated
653.74/Brazil/G5701/W. R. West
624.64/New Hampshire/G3125/
P. H. Burroughs/star sphere
357.95/Brazil/G4205
355.67/Brazil/G4204
353.63/North Carolina/G1397/
Isaac Lea Coll.
291.35/place unknown/G8253
166.76/place unknown/G8111/
M. Turetsky/star
102.18/Mexico/G4655/
Mr. & Mrs. M. O. Campbell/rutilated

Quartz (amethyst) 1362/Brazil/G3879
204.08/Brazil/G8985/I. A. Shepard
182.59/Brazil/G1272/Isaac Lea Coll.
163.84/Brazil/G8868/P. Van der Voorn
109.64/Brazil/G9575/Mr. J. W. May
96/Brazil/G5273/Mrs. G. M. Morris/
with diamond
72.18/Brazil/G9461/P. D. Cerami &
L. T. Jones
66.83/Brazil/G8638/A. Willalon
61.39/Brazil/G3914/A. R. Cutter
56/Brazil/G3165/E. Ward Copps
44.54/North Carolina/G1298/Isaac Lea Coll.
41.18/Brazil/G4355/Mr. & Mrs. J. H. Clark
36.16/Pennsylvania/G1283/Isaac Lea Coll.
33.20/North Carolina/G1288/Isaac Lea Coll.
22.90/Maine/G1271
18.71/Virginia/G1301/Isaac Lea Coll.

Quartz (ametrine) 443/Bolivia/G9220/
T. Spall, Jr.
138.74/Bolivia/G9251/R. W. Brink
55.68/Bolivia/G9576/J. W. May
24.15/Bolivia/G9950/R. Meisenhalder

Quartz (citrine) 2277/Brazil/G9742/
  D. Tepper
1180/Brazil/G1870/F. L. Chamberlain
781.44/Brazil/G3640/L. T. Chamberlain
636.55/Brazil/G7721/B. E. Ashley
469/Brazil/G8127/K. M. Kupper
277.87/Brazil/G3732/A. R. Cutter
264.74/Brazil/G2041/W. A. Roebling
226.85/Brazil/G3718/A. R. Cutter
217.50/Brazil/G4199/A. R. Cutter
169.01/Australia/G1373
156.24/place unknown/G9776
143.33/Colorado/G0456/Isaac Lea Coll.
120.32/Brazil/G2116/L. T. Chamberlain
114.60/Brazil/G3932
90.50/Brazil/G3615/A. R. Cutter
85.28/Brazil/G4915/W. Mason
78.80/Brazil/G3621/A. R. Cutter
69.50/Brazil/G4288/H. C. Hurlburt
55.49/Maine/G2178/L. T. Chamberlain
48.35/Brazil/G3915/A. R. Cutter
42.75/Brazil/G3719/A. R. Cutter

Quartz (rose) 1797.40/Brazil/G9913/
  L. T. Chamberlain/star sphere
914.90/Brazil/G4264/F. M. Hueber/star sphere
374.85/Brazil/G3592/L. T. Chamberlain
110.60/Brazil/G8861/R. W. F. Conway
83.95/Brazil/G3421

Quartz (smoky) 4570/California/G3738/
  L. T. Chamberlain/faceted egg
1695.50/Brazil/G3697/L. T. Chamberlain
163.44/Colorado/G1336
144.94/Scotland/G3079/W. A. Roebling
89.97/Switzerland/G3293
80/Arkansas/G1334
62.98/Maine/G1338
59.81/Brazil/G9015/Mrs. H. B. Berman
32.02/New Hampshire/G3124/P. H. Burroughs

Rhodochrosite 27.80/South Africa/G8871/
  J. S. Hayward
21.33/South Africa/G8454/
  Dr. & Mrs. C. C. Chiu
20.78/South Africa/G4920
15.16/South Africa/G4940
13.35/South Africa/G8919/C. Entenmann
11.22/Argentina/G8065/H. I. Saul

Rhodonite 4.89/Australia/G8039

Sanidine 15.43/Germany/G9954/
  L. T. Chamberlain

Scapolite 288.09/Burma/G3783
176.74/Tanzania/G8983/Dr. & Mrs. Y. T. Tan
103.51/Tanzania/G7348
73.31/Tanzania/G8491/
  Mr. & Mrs. R. F. Gill, Jr.
29.93/Burma/G3301/L. T. Chamberlain/
  cat's eye
26.84/Sri Lanka/G9984/F. A. Canfield/
  cat's eye
14.19/Sri Lanka/G9983/F. A. Canfield/star
12.35/Burma/G3674/L. T. Chamberlain
8.34/Tanzania/G8604/E. J. Cunningham

3.29/Burma/G2161/L. T. Chamberlain/
  cat's eye

Scheelite 48.50/California/G5115
37.04/California/G8636/A. A. Rasch
37/California/G3701/L. T. Chamberlain
19.75/Korea/G6814/R. Swabe
12.40/Arizona/G3803/W. A. Roebling
7.35/Mexico/G3731/L. T. Chamberlain

Scorodite 2.60/Namibia/G3793

Sellaite 7.17/Brazil/G9979/W. A. Roebling

Serandite 1.85/Canada/G9226/
  Mr. & Mrs. C. H. Weber, Jr.

Sillimanite 24.87/Sri Lanka/G9915

Sinhalite 109.80/Sri Lanka/G3587
43.50/Sri Lanka/G3548/L. T. Chamberlain
36.40/Sri Lanka/G8130/Dr. & Mrs. C. C.
  Chiu

Smithsonite 177.31/Namibia/G9022/
  Bay Shore Group
32.52/Namibia/G8637/A. A. Rasch
4.85/Namibia/G8820

Sodalite 8.68/place unknown/G6180/
  L. T. Chamberlain
2.29/Canada/G9948/hackmanite

Spessartine 265.85/Brazil/G8632/
  L. F. Stornelli
108.90/Brazil/G4203
53.83/Brazil/G3229/L. T. Chamberlain
40.12/Virginia/G0147/L. T. Chamberlain
27.36/Kenya/G8902/C. Entenmann
26.02/Virginia/G3597/L. T. Chamberlain
18.92/Kenya/G8866/
  Mr. & Mrs. H. K. Hecker

Sphalerite 87.87/Spain/G9018/
  Bay Shore Group
73.30/Utah/G3556
59.50/New Jersey/G3874/W. A. Roebling
48/Mexico/G2167/L. T. Chamberlain
45.90/Spain/G3707/L. T. Chamberlain
18.50/Utah/G3555/L. T. Chamberlain

Spinel 45.82/Sri Lanka/G2180/
  L. T. Chamberlain
36.10/Burma/G3685
34.07/Burma/G3354/L. T. Chamberlain
30/Burma/G3344/L. T. Chamberlain
29.70/Sri Lanka/G2165/L. T. Chamberlain
25.50/Burma/G3593/L. T. Chamberlain
22.20/Sri Lanka/G2166/L. T. Chamberlain
22.10/Sri Lanka/G2247/W. A. Roebling
13.65/Sri Lanka/G2138
8.34/place unknown/G2242/W. A. Roebling
6.65/Sri Lanka/G2255/W. A. Roebling/star

Spodumene 327.79/Brazil/G3396/
  W. A. Roebling
77.03/Afghanistan/G8446/K. Kawaoka

75.25/Brazil/G8864/Mr. & Mrs. H. K. Hecker
71.05/Madagascar /G3698/L. T. Chamberlain
68.66/Brazil/G3885/W. A. Roebling
62.59/Brazil/G9987/M. Meisenhalder
44.94/Brazil/G2163/L. T. Chamberlain
13.95/Brazil/G9732/L. Sonier/green
6.20/Brazil/G9735/L. Sonier/green
0.22, 0.37, 0.68, 0.70/North Carolina/
  G0255-258/L. T. Chamberlain/hiddenite

Spodumene (kunzite) 80.01/Brazil/G3940
396.30/Brazil/G9956/Tiffany & Co./
  Paloma Picasso necklace
372/place unknown/G9905/C. R. Read, Sr.
287.80/Brazil/G6187/
  Mr. & Mrs. D. C. Harrold
266.14/Madagascar/G8875/T. Warshaw
256/Brazil/G9155/G. Morigi
255.80/Brazil/G3429/W. A. Roebling
170.55/California/G3797/
  American Gem Society
163.89/Afghanistan/G8423/
  Mr. & Mrs. D. S. Smith
60.68/California/G1915/L. T. Chamberlain

Staurolite 3/Brazil/G3795
1.60/Brazil/G3794

Stibiotantalite 7.31/Brazil/G4917/
  L. T. Chamberlain
2.47/Mozambique/G3218/F. A. Canfield

Sugilite 23.46/South Africa/G9664/
  Royal Azel Inc.
5.03/South Africa/G9861/Royal Lavulite Inc.

Taafeite 5.34/Sri Lanka/G4509/
  F. C. Kennedy

Titanite 14.37/Madagascar/G9721
6.35/Madagascar/G8818
5.59/Mexico/G3290/W. A. Roebling
5.18/Mexico/G3292/L. T. Chamberlain
2.20/Mexico/G8814/chrome
9.33tw/Switzerland/G2043/N. Lea

Topaz 22892.50/Brazil/G9875/AFMS & Drs.
  M. & E. Borgatta/"American Golden"
12555/Brazil/G8053/faceted sphere
7725/Brazil/G3976
7033/Brazil/G8990/EDUSCO
  Investments Co./irradiated
3273/Brazil/G3633
2470/Brazil/G9242/J. M. Craver/irradiated
1174.30/Brazil/G8932/C. Entenmann/
  irradiated
815.60/Russia/G9564/L. T. Chamberlain
571.45/Brazil/G9569/C. R. Hatcher, Jr./
  irradiated
422.50/place unknown/G8890/C. Entenmann
296.56/Russia/G5004
291.50/place unknown/G9907/
  C. R. Read, Sr.
259.90/Brazil/G9140/P. Gutlohn
234.60/Colorado/G3309/L. T. Chamberlain
187.23/Brazil/G3612/A. R. Cutter
181.49/Russia/G9246/P. Van derVoorn

170.65/Madagascar/G3890
155.47/Russia/G0262
146.43/Texas/G3625/L. T. Chamberlain
129.10/Brazil/G3550/golden
93.63/Brazil/G3401/W. A. Roebling/golden
77.09/Brazil/G4916/Dr. & Mrs.
  B. A. Berman/golden
54.37/Brazil/G2219/L. T. Chamberlain
50.79/Japan/G0268
50/California/G5668/M. W. van der Velde
43.75/Maine/G2047/L. T. Chamberlain
41.24/Brazil/G2174/
  L. T. Chamberlain/golden
34.09/Brazil/G2046/L. T. Chamberlain
34.06/Brazil/G2232/L. T. Chamberlain/pink
24.35/New Hampshire/G3307/
  L. T. Chamberlain
18.12/Japan/G1178
16.97/California/G3679/E. Ware

Uvite 41.55/Sri Lanka/G3245/
  L. T. Chamberlain
10.70/Kenya/G8462/Dr. & Mrs. C. C. Chiu

Vesuvianite 7.05/Tanzania/G4937/
  L. T. Chamberlain

Willemite 11.66/New Jersey/G1898/
  L. T. Chamberlain
11.05/New Jersey/G4187

Wollastonite 1.22/Canada/G9666/
  A. T. Grant

Wulfenite 46.09/Namibia/G8067/H. I. Saul
15.70/Namibia/G7826
8.65/Mexico/G8872/C. Krotki
6.05/Arizona/G9973/L. T. Chamberlain
3.70/Namibia/G5119

Zincite 20.06/New Jersey/G3386/
  W. A. Roebling
12.32/New Jersey/G3002/W. A. Roebling

Zircon 118.01/Sri Lanka/G2236/
  W. A. Roebling
106.14/Thailand/G3568
103.16/Thailand/G2222/W. A. Roebling
97.62/Sri Lanka/G2237/W. A. Roebling
75.79/Burma/G3068/L. T. Chamberlain
64.15/Thailand/G3397/W. A. Roebling
51.29/Sri Lanka/G1179/F. L. Chamberlain
49.18/Thailand/G3394/W. A. Roebling
48.26/Sri Lanka/G3554/L. T. Chamberlain
28.08/Thailand/G2173/L. T. Chamberlain
23.41/Sri Lanka/G2233/W. A. Roebling

Zoisite (tanzanite) 122.74/Tanzania/G4876
18.16/Tanzania/G4584/
  L. T. Chamberlain/cat's eye

ACKNOWLEDGMENTS

The preparation of this book would not have been possible without the enthusiastic assistance and support of many colleagues and friends. Russell Feather, collection manager and gemologist at the National Museum of Natural History, reviewed the manuscript and was a much appreciated adviser on all aspects of the book. Christine Webb provided invaluable assistance with research, organizing photographic images, reviewing text, and cheerfully doing whatever needed to get done.

Others that contributed significantly to the project are: Linda Welzenbach, Carolyn Margolis, Linda Deck, Lee Bailey, Robert Sullivan, T. C. Benson, Mary Crowley, Sharon Barry, Daphne Ross, Paul Pohwat, Elizabeth Munsteen, and James Becker.

I very much enjoyed my collaboration with Eric Himmel, senior editor, and Carol Robson, designer, at Harry N. Abrams, Inc. Their skills, patience, and enthusiasm made the process of turning a manuscript and a set of images into a finished book both interesting and pleasurable.

Finally, this book would never have been completed without the love and patience of my wife, Ann. She reviewed text and spent hundreds of hours of quality time with our daughter, Alison, while her husband worked on the book.

PHOTOGRAPH CREDITS

All of the photographs of gems in this book were taken by Chip Clark, with the exception of the following:

Russell Feather: 121 (top)

Tino Hammid: 27 (right and bottom)

Laurie Minor-Penland: 50, 85 (top), 107 (right)

Dane Penland: 20, 29 (right), 37 (right), 52 (center and right), 70, 88, 101 (top), 102 (top), 105, 110, 119 (bottom)

Documentary photographs come from the following sources with grateful acknowledgment:

Alfred Eisenstaedt, *Life Magazine*, © Time Inc.: 19 (right)

Peter Heaney: 79

Eleona and Herbert Horovitz: 25 (center)

Kunsthistorisches Museum, Vienna: 33 (top)

Dr. Alex C. McClaren, Research School of Earth Sciences, Australian National University, Canberra: 114

Robert Morgan Studio, courtesy The Historical Society, Palm Beach County, Florida: 31 (bottom)

Museum of Modern Art Film Stills Archive, New York: 122

National Portrait Gallery, London: 25 (bottom)

Prof. H.-U. Nissen, Laboratorium für Festkorperphysik, Zurich: 115

Smithsonian Institution Archives: 17

Joanna T. Steichen: 36

Tiffany & Company: 38 (bottom), 39 (bottom)

U. S. Geological Survey Library, Reston, Virginia: 25 (top right)